History of Germany

A Captivating Guide to German History, Starting from 1871 through the First World War, Weimar Republic, and World War II to the Present

Free Bonus from Captivating History (Available for a Limited time)

Hi History Lovers!

Now you have a chance to join our exclusive history list so you can get your first history ebook for free as well as discounts and a potential to get more history books for free! Simply visit the link below to join.

Captivatinghistory.com/ebook

Also, make sure to follow us on Facebook, Twitter and Youtube by searching for Captivating History.

Contents

INTRODUCTION 1

CHAPTER 1 - PRUSSIA 4

CHAPTER 2 - THE IRON CHANCELLOR 11

CHAPTER 3 - WILHELM'S GERMANY 37

CHAPTER 4 - THE GREAT WAR 58

CHAPTER 5 - THE TREATY OF VERSAILLES 90

CHAPTER 6 - THE WEIMAR REPUBLIC 100

CHAPTER 7 - HITLER, ANTI-SEMITISM, AND THE RISE OF T
HE NAZIS 120

CHAPTER 8 - THE NAZIS TAKE POWER.................................. 139

CHAPTER 9 - THE NAZIS IN POWER 147

CHAPTER 10 - THE HOLOCAUST... 202

CHAPTER 11 - POST-WAR GERMANY TO THE PRESENT DAY 217

CONCLUSION 230

HERE'S ANOTHER BOOK BY CAPTIVATING HISTORY
THAT YOU MIGHT LIKE.. 232

FREE BONUS FROM CAPTIVATING HISTORY (AVAILABLE
FOR A LIMITED TIME).. 233

BIBLIOGRAPHY/REFERENCES 234

Introduction

The United States is a nation, mostly of people descended from or who are immigrants. Of the over 330 million people who live in the country as of 2021, about 16 percent of them claim some German heritage, which is more than any other ethnic group. This is surprising considering the nation was founded primarily by English colonists and whose Irish-descended population is greater than the population of Ireland itself.

Most of the German immigrants to the United States arrived before World War I, and many arrived before 1871. The year 1871 seems like a sort of arbitrary date until you know that the modern nation state of Germany was founded in that year. Strictly speaking, many of the German immigrants to the US were not really German at all—they were Swiss, Bavarians, Alsatians, Westphalians, or one of the many other German states that existed before the country was united behind its most powerful kingdom, Prussia.

Perhaps the most famous group of German immigrants in the United States are the Amish and Mennonites of Pennsylvania, erroneously called the "Pennsylvania Dutch." They are not "Dutch" (as in from the Netherlands/Holland) but German, with "Deutsch" being the German word for themselves. Americans heard a dialect of German, and to them, it sounded like "Dutch," not "doi-ch" (as one might pronounce the name phonetically).

Illustration 1: Map of German States, 1864–1871

As you may know, the Amish and Mennonites ("Amish" is derived from early leader Jakob Amman of Switzerland and "Mennonite" comes from Menno Simons, the leader of that sect) of the US, whether they live in Pennsylvania or elsewhere, came to the United States fleeing persecution in their home country, like many other people coming to North America. However, while the "Pennsylvania Dutch" were, in a sense, persecuted for their religion, it was one aspect of their religious beliefs that caused their persecution back in Europe—their belief in pacifism. They were opposed to war, and in the Germany of the late 17th to early 19th centuries, war was almost as common as breathing.

The Amish and Mennonites refused to be drafted into the various armies of the states they lived in, sometimes resulting in very harsh sentences, both economic and physical (jail, beatings, etc.). One way they protested and set themselves apart was the growing of beards *without* mustaches; throughout the 17th to 19th centuries, the military men of Europe, particularly in the German states, wore very bushy and elaborate mustaches. The absence of hair under the nose was an obvious "up yours" to the authorities.

As you can see from the map on the previous page, what is now Germany was divided into many principalities, kingdoms, duchies, and bishoprics (governed by a bishop of the Catholic Church). Prior to Napoleon Bonaparte's invasions, there were, at times, nearly three hundred different German entities, but in the time that concerns us, 1864 (when the push for German unity behind Prussia began) to 1871 (when unity was achieved under the Prussian royal house, the Hohenzollerns), there were thirty-nine states.

A quick look at the map above will tell you that there were four more dominant German-speaking entities in the middle of Europe. These were the Austrian Empire, Prussia, Bavaria, and, lastly, Hanover (the present-day British monarchy comes from the House of Hanover, starting with George I in 1714). Of these four, the Prussians and Austrians were the strongest and most influential, and it is with the conflict of these two kingdoms that our story will begin.

Chapter 1 – Prussia

The modern nation of Germany coalesced around the powerful eastern German state of Prussia in 1870/1871. If you could go back in time and visit Prussia in 1617, you might be shocked that this relatively poor and poorly situated kingdom would be the seed around which Germany would grow.

Prussia's soil was not the greatest, and even the great estates of the kingdom sometimes struggled to provide enough crops for food or trade. Rye, sugar beets, and potatoes were the chief crops. As far as the raw materials needed for a modern economy, Prussia itself had virtually none. It gained some coal reserves with the annexation of Silesia in 1741, and it gained access to much larger quantities in the early 1800s with the addition of lands on the Rhine River and to its immediate south when it was given control of them during the Congress of Vienna after the Napoleonic Wars.

The royal family of Prussia had begun as the Margraves (a unique title within the Holy Roman Empire) of Brandenburg in 1417 with Frederick I, Elector of Brandenburg (an "elector" theoretically had a say in the naming of the Holy Roman Emperor). The capital of the Margravate of Brandenburg was a small city (more a large town) called Berlin.

In 1518, the Hohenzollern family ascended to rule Brandenburg, which had slowly been enlarged over the past century by marriage unions and shrewd negotiations with smaller duchies on its borders. In 1618, the electors of Brandenburg became rulers of the larger (but poorer) neighboring state of Prussia. The kings of Prussia were of another branch of the Hohenzollern family, and in 1618, the branches came together with Johannes Sigismund, who died in 1619. He passed the throne to his son, Georg Wilhelm (r. 1619-1640).

Georg Wilhelm was an ineffective king who lived at an unfortunate time. He reigned through most of the incredibly bloody Thirty Years' War, and both he and Prussia only narrowly survived a time in which some part of what is now Germany lost more than half of its population due to war, famine, and disease.

Prussia (officially Brandenburg-Prussia) was fortunate that Georg Wilhelm's heir, Frederick William (r. 1640-1688), was a much more intelligent and accomplished ruler.

(You will note throughout this book that at times, the spelling of names will change from the German spelling, as in the case of "Georg Wilhelm," to English, as in the case of "Frederick William." It's just the convention, depending on the person. The greatest Prussian king was "Frederick the Great," but you never see it as the German "Friedrich der Große" in English language books. On the other hand, you rarely see the name of the last German king, "Kaiser Wilhelm II," written as "Emperor William II." Also, please note that the unique German letter "ß" acts just like a double "s.")

Frederick promoted the growth of a middle trading class in his lands, and the Prussian economy during his reign began to grow beyond what it had been for centuries, the home of large agricultural estates. These estates and the men who owned them (most often military men) were the backbone of support for the king, which continued until the abdication of Kaiser Wilhelm II in 1918. This Prussian ruling class is known by the collective name of

"Junkers" (which originally meant "young lord" or "country squire" but which became associated with the strict disciplined military men that ruled the area and which formed the backbone for the Prussian, and later German, officer class).

Among Frederick's many reforms were changes in the army. During his rule, Frederick developed one of the first standing armies in Europe and instituted the method in which German field commanders were given wide latitude in achieving their objectives. This military doctrine truly began in Prussia, and it continued into World Wars I and II and lives on not only in the German Army today but in most of the world's armed forces.

During the reign of Frederick William, the Prussians first came to the fore as a military power to be reckoned with. Fighting in the Second Northern War with Sweden (then a great regional power) against the Poles and Lithuanians (then a great power in decline), Frederick William won the Battle of Warsaw with the Swedes and then turned and defeated the Swedes a short time later when they switched sides against him. At the time (1678), this shocked many in Europe, for the Swedes had a fearsome reputation.

Frederick William's successor, Frederick I, ruled from 1701 to 1713 and was a noted soldier, taking part as a field commander in wars against King Louis XIV of France. During the reign of Frederick I, Prussia officially became a kingdom within the Holy Roman Empire (centered in Vienna, with the Austrian emperor as its head), though it took much political maneuvering to do so, as there were supposed to be no independent kings within the empire. Frederick I settled for the title "King in Prussia." His more famous and accomplished grandson, Frederick II, better known as Frederick the Great, felt strong enough to declare himself "King of Prussia."

Expansion of PRUSSIA 1807-1871

PRUSSIA

Prussian territory 1793-1807, ceded to Russia 1815

Prussian territory after the Treaty of Tilsit, 1807

Territory gained or regained, 1815

Territory gained after Danish and Austrian wars, 1863-66

States joining the German Empire, 1871

Seized from France, 1871

To Prussia, 1849

1 Alsace-Lorraine
2 Baden
3 Bavaria
4 Hanover
5 Hesse
6 Hesse-Nassau
7 Hohenzollern
8 Holstein
9 Mecklenburg
10 Oldenburg
11 Posen
12 Rhine Province
13 Saxony
14 Schleswig
15 Swedish Pomerania
16 Westphalia
17 Wurttemburg

Frederick William I (r. 1713-1740) is often referred to as the "Military King," for it was he who made the Prussian Army into the central institution of Prussian life. Though he is known for the role he played in growing Prussia's army, Frederick William I also did much for the country economically. He began land reclamation projects, which increased the amount of arable land in the country, reformed the tax system, improved roads, and streamlined an already impressive civil service system. He also began building schools and hospitals that were more accessible to the common people than just those at the top.

Unfortunately, many of Frederick William's better accomplishments have been overshadowed by two things, one of them relatively trivial and the other more consequential.

First, the trivial. Frederick William I was fascinated by all things military. This interest ran the gamut from actual battles and weaponry to the pomp of the parade ground. Somewhere in between is Frederick's most noted "accomplishment": he wanted to form a guard unit of the largest men he could find. This unit was Prussian infantry regiment number six, better known to history as the Potsdam Giants, named for the location of Frederick William's palace. Many of the "Giants" were not even Prussian. Most of them were, but a significant number came from other German states, induced by offers of good pay, and a number came from foreign countries, whose leaders sent Frederick William taller than average men for his unit as a goodwill gesture. Not all of these men went willingly, and some deserted. Additionally, quite a few of the Giants were literally dragged off the street or threatened if they didn't join. Making the story even stranger was the king's attempts to pair his Giants off with tall women to create a "race of giants," which he would use as his shock troops. This effort, with its foreshadowing of Nazi attempts at genetic engineering, amounted to virtually nothing.

More consequential in the long run was Frederick William's relationship with his son, Frederick (what else?), who became the famous Frederick the Great. At first, the king loved his son and doted upon him, but as Frederick II grew up, the king and the prince found they had virtually nothing in common.

Frederick II was not interested in military affairs to anything close to the degree his father was, which is strange considering he became one of the greatest military leaders Europe has ever seen. This enraged his father, who denigrated and likely beat his son frequently. Frederick II had a sentimental soul, and while he was forced to learn the military arts, he gravitated toward music, writing, and the theater. At one point in his late teens, Frederick, who would later marry a German princess, had a homosexual relationship with one of the king's pages. This was found out. The page was sent to military duty far away, and Frederick was forced to live in isolation for a time at one of his father's lodges to meditate on his "sin." Another same-sex relationship was found out later, and though this was kept relatively quiet, the prince suffered greatly, including being thrown in prison for a time by order of his father. Frederick and his wife, Elisabeth, spent much time apart and had no children, leading most historians to believe that he was primarily homosexual in his sexual life.

Regardless, Frederick was the sole male heir and became king when his father died in 1740. He reigned for forty-six years, the longest-reigning king of any of the Hohenzollerns of Prussia/Germany.

During his long reign, Frederick continued the tradition of a standing Prussian army and instituted a variety of reforms to make the army more responsive on the battlefield. He kept up with all military matters throughout Europe and kept his troops supplied with the latest weapons. Over the course of his reign, Frederick defeated a number of European countries, sometimes in concert with allies and sometimes alone against great odds. His campaigns were marked by speed, audacity, discipline, and great leadership (both on his part and on the part of the men he placed in command). The man that Napoleon Bonaparte looked up to as his military hero was none other than Frederick the Great.

Frederick was not only known for his military prowess but also for his expansive intellect. Known as one of the most "enlightened" rulers of the Enlightenment, Frederick spoke, wrote, and read French fluently and kept abreast of the thinking of great philosophers such as Voltaire, with whom he formed a personal friendship. He invited painters, architects, musicians, sculptors, and writers to Prussia and commissioned works by many of the great names of the period. He was also an accomplished musician.

However, while Frederick II was not the harsh king his father had been, his enlightened thinking only went so far. He kept firm control of power in his country and suppressed any movements toward a more liberal form of government.

Unfortunately for Prussia, much of the first half of the 19th century saw a decline, both economically and, most importantly, militarily. During the reign of Napoleon, Prussia became a French satellite state until it turned on the French emperor following his disastrous campaign in Russia and then in Waterloo.

It took decades for Prussia to recover from the early part of the 1800s, but in 1862, when a new chancellor was named by King Wilhelm I, the kingdom had regained much of its economic strength, was continuing to develop militarily, and wanted to be able to compete with its stronger European neighbors (primarily France, Austria, and England) on the world stage.

Chapter 2 – The Iron Chancellor

The Prussian monarchy gained a new king in 1861 with the death of Frederick William IV (r. 1840–1861) and the ascension of his brother, Wilhelm I (r. 1861–1888), but in a land where the rule of the king was virtually absolute, it was not Wilhelm that created a united Germany but his chancellor, Otto von Bismarck, known to history as the "Iron Chancellor." That name fits perfectly, for Bismarck was a man who knew what he wanted, knew how to go about getting it, and was only mildly bothered by the human cost it took to get it.

Bismarck was of the land-owning Junker class of Prussia. By the time of his political rise, the Junkers had essentially been ruling Prussia for centuries under the king. Before we go into Bismarck, his history, and his role in the unification of Germany, let's talk just a bit about the Junkers.

When WWI ended, Germany became a democracy with virtually full freedom of expression. Intellectuals and artists of all kinds lampooned the Junker class as outdated examples of tin-pot martinets who obeyed orders on command and who marched on the Kaiser's enemies like wind-up soldiers goose-stepping in one direction until pushed in another. After the bloodshed of WWI, which many in Germany (from the far left to the moderate right) blamed on the Junker class, the Junkers became a sort of laughing stock, set up as examples of mindless automatons, but there was far more to them than just obedience.

The Junker class and the officers of the German military in general (and most of the generals of the pre-WWII army were Junkers) lived by the same sort of ethos that the Japanese samurai were famous for (the Bushido code). The Junker code did emphasize obedience to one's superiors (whether in military rank or by birth) in the same way as its Japanese counterpart did. It also stressed acting in an "honorable" way, though this usually boiled down to obedience, regardless of belief, and keeping one's word. Discipline and stoicism were emphasized, and if there was ever a place where the old saying "Spare the rod and spoil the child" was practiced perhaps more than preached, it was Prussia. Generally speaking, children (especially sons) could expect harsh physical punishments at the slightest infractions—this, among other things, was thought to "toughen them up," for there were only two possible futures for the sons of the Junker class (or at least for the eldest son): landowners or the military, although they usually engaged in both. Other sons might be expected to become pastors, lawyers, or civil servants (or all three).

Duty to the Kaiser and the country was paramount. The individual came a distant second. This was the unspoken creed of the Junker class.

Many if not most of the Junkers governed large estates, sometimes with hundreds of workers on them. These workers were akin to enslaved people in many ways. Until the second half of the 19th century, virtually all the laborers/peasants born on an estate were tied there—they could never leave, at least not without express permission. The discipline meted out to the sons of the Junkers paled in comparison to that meted out to peasants who disobeyed, attempted to flee, or committed any number of infractions (many of which depended on the whim of the landowner). Flogging, being placed in the stocks, and/or exposed to cold weather were just some of the methods used to keep "order" on the estate. Of course, not all Junkers were this harsh, and many of them allowed their workers a modicum of freedom, but still, it was not "freedom" as we think of it today.

At times, even today, political and other cartoons lampoon a politician, policeman, or father who is particularly hard-headed and stupid as a "Junker," and many times, the person being made fun of is wearing the famous Pickelhaube, the "pointed bonnet" worn by the German Army until mid-way through WWI by its General Staff.

Illustration 2: Otto von Bismarck wearing an elaborate "pickelhaube" for this formal portrait taken after 1870.

Though many Junkers could be thick-headed obtuse martinets, many obviously were not. Though the martial arts (and in this case, we are referring to anything to do with combat and war, not karate) were emphasized before all else, many of the Junker class were musically trained and well-read intellectuals. If the Prussian Army had been led solely by dull-witted robots, it would not have become the highly skilled force that it developed into under Frederick the Great.

The power of the Junkers was so profound that, at least in their locality, they could override the decision of judges and easily sway what little representative bodies there might be in towns and cities. If you belonged to a great Junker family or were of a high rank (many times one and the same), your word was essentially law, especially in the area around your estates.

The Prussian Army, and then German Army, was sometimes compared to that of a machine moving in perfect time, each part doing exactly what it was supposed to do, but it should be remembered that from the time of Frederick the Great, independent thinking was encouraged in the Prussian Army. This did not mean that an officer could do whatever he wanted, but generally speaking, once he was given an objective, he was free to come up with his own plan for achieving it. Of course, many times, this plan had to be approved, but on the battlefield, where decisions had to be made on the spot, a Prussian officer was given amazing leeway, likely more than in any army in the world at the time. This leeway did not just apply to generals, as it continued down the chain of command, all the way down to sergeants or corporals.

At the platoon level (about forty men, give or take), sergeants were given a task and many times were asked to devise a plan for carrying it out. This did not happen all the time, and the freedom given to a non-commissioned officer paled to that given to a captain or colonel, for example, but it was a regular feature of the Prussian war machine. Additionally, a corporal was expected to know the requirements and duties of the rank above him (sergeant), the sergeant those of the lieutenant, the lieutenant the captain's, and so on. Thus, should a man fall on the field, his replacement would know what was expected of him.

Today, these two features of the Prussian military don't seem so special or unique because virtually all modern armies have adopted them. It began with the Prussians/Germans, as did the idea of a general staff and much else, including the foundation of modern camouflage theory.

Otto von Bismarck was born on April 1ˢᵗ, 1815, in Schönhausen. In 1865, he was made a count (*Graf*), and in 1871, after his efforts had unified Germany under the Prussian king, he was given the title "prince" (*Fürst*). And, on top of that, in 1890, two years after he had been forced into retirement by the new Kaiser, Wilhelm II, he was made duke (*Herzog*) of Lauenburg, a duchy on the Danish border that had been acquired in one of the wars of German unification.

Bismarck's family had been given lands and nobility five generations before the birth of Otto in 1815. His father, Karl Wilhelm Ferdinand von Bismarck, had been a military officer, and his mother came from well-known families on both sides. Bismarck was the middle child, and he had an older brother and a younger sister. The Bismarcks' ancestral estate is located in Poland today, a result of the border changes that took place after WWII.

Bismarck was highly educated and highly intelligent, and he entered the University of Göttingen (in today's central Germany) and studied law. Throughout his life, Bismarck knew the value of being underestimated. While he was sometimes outspoken and convinced he was right, he also allowed people to form their own image of him by keeping quiet, and in later years, he almost always wore a military uniform, both to show his commitment to the armed forces and to promote the idea that he was simply another dull-witted robotic Junker.

He most definitely was not dull-witted. He spoke five languages and was able to engage almost everyone he met on equal terms on subjects ranging from government to the arts and philosophy. Bismarck's dream in college was to gain a prestigious law degree to become a diplomat, which he saw as a way to both travel and gain influence.

Bismarck, like many of those who recognize they are gifted with abilities far beyond the average person, developed the somewhat "un-Prussian" habit of doing what he wanted when he wanted to do it. He put his apprenticeship in jeopardy by disappearing for a time, chasing after two aristocratic young English women. In his younger years, Bismarck had no use for religion, but after becoming acquainted (in the most platonic sense) with his best friend's wife, he became a devout Lutheran and considered religion as a pillar of the Prussian state.

Like most other young men of his class, Bismarck served for a time in the army and then the reserves. He returned to Schönhausen in 1839 to run the family estate when his mother died. His father had no skill in farming or running a large estate, not to mention little interest. It fell to Otto to govern the estate and set it back on its feet, which he managed to do in very little time.

In 1847, he married Johanna von Puttkamer, who hailed from another Junker family (one of her distant relatives was an admiral under Adolf Hitler and was wounded in the 1944 assassination attempt against him), and she bore Otto three children. By all accounts, his marriage was a happy one from beginning to end.

In the same year, Bismarck was elected to the Prussian parliament (the Landtag). This newly formed body, a reaction to many of the changes that took place in Europe after the French Revolution, held little power, but in 1848, as revolution spread throughout Europe once again, more liberal legislators in the Landtag pushed for a variety of reforms. Bismarck came to the attention of the Kaiser (at that time, Frederick William IV) and those around him for the conservative, reactionary stance he took against the liberals during that tumultuous year.

Within two years, Bismarck was appointed as the ambassador to the German Confederation (a body representing all the German-speaking states, including Austria), then Russia, and finally France. These positions gave him a wide knowledge of events in these countries, a wide circle of friends and acquaintances, and an idea of these nations' foreign policy goals.

During his years as ambassador, Bismarck's reports, insights, and personality made him a noted figure in Prussian politics. Wilhelm I appointed Bismarck as the chancellor in 1862, one year after taking the throne. Bismarck's insight into political matters in Prussia, the other German states, and most of Europe (including Prussia's most likely rivals on the Continent—Russia, France, and Austria) made him the man for the job. While Wilhelm was not a stupid man, he was also not Bismarck, and he preferred to reign rather than rule unless there was a particular item or affair that interested or troubled him. In many cases, Bismarck and the king saw eye to eye, but when they didn't, Bismarck was often able to successfully argue his case to the king. If that did not work, the chancellor was not above manipulation and secrecy. At times, as he became more and more indispensable, he was known to throw a tantrum or two, but he knew exactly when to stop before he crossed a line.

Bismarck realized that for Prussia to really flourish, it would have to expand, and the only realistic way for it to do that was to unify the smaller German states around it. To the east of the country lay Russia, and as powerful as the Prussian Army was and would become, a war with Russia over lands that were not German to begin with was a losing proposition.

In the south lay the other major German-speaking power, Austria. While leaders of both kingdoms had at times bandied about the idea of the unification of Austria and Prussia, there were a number of quite obvious reasons it would not work. The first was who would be the head of the country? Neither sovereign wanted to play second fiddle, and history had shown that the idea of co-rulers was doomed to failure.

Secondly, Austria was a Catholic kingdom, the home of the Holy Roman Empire (the title of Holy Roman emperor, while having some meaning when Charlemagne became the first Holy Roman emperor in 800 CE, was essentially a meaningless title bestowed by the pope just a relatively short time after Charlemagne). Prussia and the lands it controlled in northern Germany were predominantly Protestant. Long and extraordinarily bloody wars had been fought in Germany over religion in the not-too-distant past, and no one was ready to live under a "heretical" monarch.

Thirdly, the other powers of Europe had made it quite clear that no union between Austria and Prussia could or would be tolerated. A huge German-speaking empire in the center of Europe would be too powerful and threaten the interests of nearly all of Europe.

Bismarck was quite aware of all these matters. He wasn't the only Prussian to understand that the German states were the only place for Prussia to expand, but he was essentially the only one with an idea of how it could be accomplished. And he had the power and position to set things in motion.

While Bismarck had a notion of how to achieve his goals, he also knew he was dependent on circumstances and how to take advantage of them. His first opportunity came in 1864 when the Danish king, Fredrick VII, died in 1863.

In 1863, the Danes were a relatively liberal monarchy, but they still hung onto the idea of an empire. At various times throughout history, Danish kings controlled England, Norway, and Denmark, parts of southern Sweden, and/or the German coast. However, in 1863, Denmark was no longer a power to be reckoned with to any great degree, except for the fact that the Danish king personally owned the two duchies (ruled by the king as "duke") of Schleswig and Holstein, which were populated by a German majority and lay between Denmark and the German states.

Denmark itself was governed as a constitutional monarchy, but the two provinces were governed as an absolute monarchy. Even many liberal Danes believed that Schleswig and Holstein both acted as a buffer between Denmark and the Germans and as the last remnants of its former glory. In addition, both states were quite rich in agriculture and shipping. They feared that if the reins of government were loosened on the two states, the population there would vote (either with ballots or swords) to join the German Confederation (the loose union of German states) or, worse, with Austria or Prussia.

Between 1848 and 1852, Denmark had successfully staved off both rebellion and outside interference over the two states in the First Schleswig War, but it was forced to agree that the two duchies were the personal property of the Danish king and his heirs, not the Danish government. When King Fredrick died, he was childless, meaning he had no direct heirs, at least in the minds of the Prussians and Austrians, who also had influence in the area, especially in the southern state of Holstein.

In 1863, the new king, Christian IX, under pressure brought by his parliament and people, unilaterally revised the previous agreement (known as the London Protocol of 1852) and retained personal control of both duchies, angering the German population of the states and giving Bismarck the excuse he needed for war. After all, the Danish king had violated an international agreement, and besides, the German population of the Danish-controlled states wanted to be free of Danish rule.

Both Prussia and Austria declared war on Denmark on January 14th, 1864. Even though the Prussians were the most vocal on the issue, the Austrians had interests in the area and could not afford to allow Prussia to gain the territories for itself. Surprisingly, a number of other smaller German states refused to go along with the war, worried that the seemingly inevitable Prusso-Austrian victory would result in the two larger states becoming even more dominant in German affairs than they already were. In a council of the German Confederation, the issue of war came down to "might makes right"— the Austrians and the Prussians were just too powerful to oppose.

The Second Schleswig War lasted just under nine months. Initially, the Danes voluntarily gave up on the southernmost state, Holstein, and retreated behind their ancient yet somewhat modernized defensive line known as the *Dannewirke* (the "Daneworks"), which had kept out invaders since the time of Charlemagne.

However, this wasn't the 9th century, and the *Dannewirke* was easily outmaneuvered, both by sea and around its flanks, which was exactly how the Prussian-Austrian forces defeated the smaller power. The Peace of Prague, signed in 1866, made official what had been already decided in combat: Denmark would lose Schleswig and Holstein. Schleswig would be given to Prussia, and Holstein would be given to Austria. About 200,000 Danes living in the duchies became citizens of the German Confederation. Within a relatively short time, most of them left for Denmark.

As you can see in the map above, this situation, with Schleswig separated from Prussia by sea and located next to Austrian territory, could prove problematic. Questions of transportation of people and goods (especially now that railroads were making travel and transport easier and faster) would pop up often. Shipping, especially in the famous Kiel Canal, also raised problems. Most diplomats and government officials would consider these questions a nightmare. Not Bismarck. As a matter of fact, the worse relations got between Austria and Prussia, the better it suited him.

This was because Bismarck saw these problems as an opportunity. During the war with Denmark, the Prussians saw exactly how backward the Austrians were compared to them. Many of their weapons were old; their organization was sloppy, outdated, and slow; and their officers (in many but not all instances) were not as good as the Prussians. Now, if only Bismarck could somehow maneuver the Austrians into declaring war on Prussia. If that happened, Prussia would have no choice but to defend itself. And should the Prussians win a victory over the Austrians, that would leave Prussia the dominant power among the German states. And that's exactly what Bismarck spent the next two years trying to do.

For many years, the prevalent belief among historians was that Bismarck engineered this entire plan, from the war with Denmark to the war with Austria and beyond. Starting in the 1990s, Bismarck's role began to be seen in a different light, with people believing that he was simply taking advantage of events as they occurred. Today, most professional historians believe that the truth falls somewhere in between, with Bismarck taking a very active role, knowing what he wanted the final outcome to be, and both riding out and steering events as they happened.

It took a little under two years for Austria and Prussia to go to war. Austria's concern that Prussia was dominating the German-speaking states and becoming too powerful in Europe. In addition to that, there was the issue of the administration of the two duchies of Schleswig and Holstein. However, what ultimately led to war was the Austrian governor of Holstein's decision in late January 1866 to let the major estate holders in *both* duchies hold an assembly. This was a unilateral decision by the Austrian government, which had promised to abide by the principle of joint sovereignty with Prussia when it came to issues concerning both territories. Not only did Prussia see this as an attempt by Austria to extend its influence into Schleswig, which had been given to Prussia in the Second Schleswig War, but also as a direct slap in Prussia' face and a test to see whether Austria could go further in their attempts to weaken Prussian influence among the lesser German states.

Austria believed it was within its rights, while Prussia did not. Throughout the intervening years, indeed since he had become chancellor, Bismarck had promoted and publicized the idea of a *Kleindeutschland* (literally "small Germany") among the many states of Germany united around and under Prussian rule as opposed to *Grossdeutschland* ("Greater Germany"), which had been advocated for decades and was centered on the Austrian Crown. Within Prussia, there was a public outcry against what was seen as Austria's move toward a *Grossdeutschland* or at least the limiting of Prussia's power and rights.

Still, Bismarck waited to see what the Austrians would do in response to Prussia's strongly worded protest. In March, he got his answer. Austria mobilized its armies on the Prussian border—the first step toward war. In late March, Prussia began a partial mobilization itself.

All the while, Bismarck sought to isolate the Austrians diplomatically. First, he secured an agreement with Italy that it would go to war with Austria should war develop between Austria and Prussia. This benefited Italy; for a number of years, the many states of Italy had been fighting a war of unification themselves, centered around the powerful state of Savoy. The largest obstacle left in the Italian struggle was to end Austrian control of several territories that were populated by an Italian majority. In the summer of 1866, Italy went to war with Austria, and though the war was essentially a stalemate, the Austrians were forced by Prussia, Italy's ally, to cede Venetia to Italy (it's a bit more complicated than that, but in the end, Italy got what it wanted).

With Italian troops mobilizing on its southern border and Prussian troops on its northern border, Austria looked to France for an alliance, but Bismarck had beaten them to it. He had approached the French leader, Napoleon III, and they met at the French resort town of Biarritz. No one is exactly sure what the two leaders discussed, but in the end, Bismarck felt that he had been promised French neutrality. He also likely knew that the French leader believed Austria would win the war, in which case France could possibly make territorial demands of a weakened Prussia in the states and cities it controlled in western Germany. If Prussia won, then Napoleon III could try to pry territorial concessions from Bismarck for staying neutral.

So, when the war began, the supposedly powerful Austrian Empire was isolated and on its own. Furthermore, its armies were divided between the north and south (admittedly, more Austrian troops faced the Prussians than the Italians), and the Prussians outnumbered the Austrians and their smaller German allies. Prussia had created the world's first general staff, a permanent body whose job was to plan for future wars in detail, prepare and set in motion mobilization plans, equip and train the standing professional army Prussia had had since the late 1600s, and much more. Austria had no such body. Each general had command of his own army, and when war broke out, a council was convened to discuss what to do. This is akin to a professional football team playing a bunch of neighborhood amateurs.

Making things worse for the Austrians and better for the Prussians was the fact that since the beginning of the century, the Prussians had been laying railroads throughout their territory. The Austrians had been very lax about railroad development. Leading to the border area between the two kingdoms, Prussia had five major railways. Austria had one. It's quite obvious the advantage in speed, concentration, and maneuvering the Prussians possessed over the Austrians.

The Prussians also put out hundreds of miles of telegraph poles and wires, whereas the Austrians had very few and relied on horse-borne communication from their various headquarters and officers to the field.

As if this weren't enough, the Prussians enjoyed a sizable advantage when it came to personal weaponry. The vast majority of Prussian infantrymen carried the Dreyse needle-gun, one of the first breech-loading bolt-action rifles in history. The name "needle-gun" came from the sharp firing pin inside the weapon, which struck the bullet. In comparison, the Austrians were still using muzzle-loading rifles, which meant that a soldier had to stand or kneel to reload the powder, cartridge, and ball into the barrel of his gun. For every round the Austrians fired, the Prussians fired four or more.

Strangely enough, the Austrians had an advantage in artillery. They possessed breech-loading cannons, whereas the Prussians were mostly equipped with muzzle-loading guns. However, though a corps of Austrian artillerymen and officers were quite proficient with their cannons, most of their men were conscripts who received little training. By contrast, the Prussian system allowed for both a standing army and a sort of national guard (men whose time in the regular army had expired but who were still required to train on a regular basis for a number of years), and these men were quite familiar with their weapons. Additionally, the Prussian advantages in mobility meant that they could bring cannons more quickly to bear than their Austrian enemies.

If it sounds to you like the Austrians were headed for a huge defeat, you would be correct, but at the start of the war, many people around the world expected the Austrians to be victorious or for the war to be protracted. Neither happened. The Austro-Prussian War was essentially over in one battle on July 3rd, 1866: the

Battle of Königgrätz (as it was known to the Prussians) or the Battle of Sadowa (as it was known to the Austrians).

Though a number of smaller battles occurred between Prussia's and Austria's allies, including a surprising Prussian defeat at the hands of the Hanoverians (which was soon avenged), the Battle of Königgrätz decided the war. While outnumbered by the Austrians, Prussian mobility and their leadership's quick thinking, along with the much greater fighting spirit of Prussia's well-trained and motivated troops, allowed them to inflict a decisive victory, causing nearly seven times the number of casualties on the Austrians as they themselves sustained. On July 22nd, the Austrians asked for a ceasefire as a preliminary to final peace talks, which resulted in the Peace of Prague, signed on August 23rd, 1866.

The consequences for Austria, Prussia, and the other German states were huge. Prussia would take control of Austria's smaller allies in Germany, Austria would no longer be involved in German affairs, and the German Confederation, a sort of "United Nations" of German-speaking states, where issues were theoretically supposed to be discussed, voted on, and solved, was ended. In its place was the North German Confederation, which was headed by Prussia.

*Illustration 3: Prussia after the Austro-Prussian War of 1866
(courtesy of Thompson Wandsworth)*

The results of the war were very clear: Prussia was the rising power in central Europe and Austria the declining power. Seemingly overnight, Austria's role in European politics essentially ended. In an attempt to shore up its strength, both internally and externally, the Austrian Crown and the powerful Hungarian minority in the empire agreed on a power-sharing agreement, and a new entity was born: the Austro-Hungarian Empire.

The popularity of both Bismarck and Kaiser Wilhelm I soared after the victory over Austria. They were to reach all-time highs after Bismarck's next move.

Historians may have doubts over Bismarck's role in propelling the events in the war with Denmark and with Austria, but there really is no doubt that Bismarck was almost solely responsible for the instigation of Prussia's war with France, the last power in Europe that could prevent a unified Germany under Prussian leadership from happening.

France's leader in 1870 was the nephew of the great Napoleon Bonaparte, Louis Napoleon Bonaparte, better known as Napoleon III (Napoleon's only son died of complications from pneumonia and tuberculosis in 1832). Napoleon III actually was in power far longer than his famous uncle, and the main reason was that he knew that if he attempted to recreate his uncle's European empire, the entire continent would have turned against him and much more rapidly than they had against his more famous predecessor. No one wanted to see a recreation of the Napoleonic empire.

France did take part in the Crimean War, allying with Great Britain against Russia, and came to the aid of Italian patriots in their war against Austria in 1859. Napoleon III also was the impetus behind France's overseas empire, which conquered or absorbed vast areas of Asia, islands in the Pacific, and a large part of Africa, but he did not attempt to expand France in Europe as his uncle had.

Napoleon III oversaw much during his time in power: the beginnings of the Suez Canal, the reconstruction of much of Paris, and the changes wrought in the economy by developing industries. For much of Napoleon III's "Second Empire," France's economy thrived, but toward the end of the 1860s, France entered an economic downturn marked by large deficits and inflation. Additionally, many people in both the government and the population at large were beginning to tire of rule by royal decree and wanted more representation and say in how their government functioned. The National Assembly, in particular, grew resentful as Napoleon III increasingly only consulted them when he needed more money to spend.

As his popularity dropped in the country, he turned more and more to sycophants and to his wife, Empress Eugénie, who, though once a relatively liberal person, turned more conservative as time went by. The people around Napoleon III began to whisper in his ear, and what they mostly had to say was that Great Britain (having the greater overseas empire) and now the rising power of Prussia were taking all of the glory and that France, which meant Louis-Napoleon as well, was being overshadowed. Louis and his coterie also knew the value of foreign distractions, both in uniting the people and getting them to overlook some of the more glaring problems in the country.

When Bismarck and Napoleon III met at Biarritz before the Austro-Prussian War, Bismarck let Louis-Napoleon believe that if there was a Prussian victory, he would be amenable to giving France land in the western German territory of the Palatinate and in Luxembourg. When the war ended, Louis-Napoleon attempted to "cash in" on his promise to Bismarck, as France had remained neutral in the war. So, Louis-Napoleon put pressure on Bismarck to give those territories to France. Just after the end of the Franco-Prussian War, Bismarck recounted his reaction to the French demands in a speech to the Reichstag (the German parliament). His response to the French ambassador, or at least what he told the Reichstag his response was, was "Good, then it's war!" The story goes that the ambassador rushed home to a sick Napoleon III, who recanted, claiming he had been "tricked" into sending the ambassador while with fever.

Regardless of whether that story is true, between 1866 and 1870, tensions became increasingly high between Prussia and France. The straw that broke the camel's back involved an issue over the succession of a new king in Spain.

In 1868, a rebellion in Spain overthrew Queen Isabella II (r. 1833–1869), whose rule became increasingly autocratic, erratic, and unpopular toward the end of her life. When she was deposed, the authorities in Spain cast about for a successor, one they hoped would rule as a more liberal and perhaps constitutional monarch. With Prussian urging, they eventually settled upon a German prince of the House of Hohenzollern (the house of the Prussian Kaiser), who had a legitimate though distant claim to the Spanish throne.

This prince, Leopold, was acceptable to the Spanish, but he was not at all acceptable to the French. In French eyes, having a Hohenzollern on the Spanish throne would mean that the rulers of the two major countries on its borders were from the same German family, which was a risk France was not willing to take. And not only did Napoleon III, his wife, and the government felt this way, but so did most of the people of France as well.

Louis-Napoleon vociferously and loudly protested the plan to place Leopold on the throne of Spain to the point of threatening war. The Prussians eventually agreed to remove his name from contention, at least for the time being. This was not enough for the French, and what happened next shows Bismarck at his most brilliant and most devious.

Talks between Kaiser Wilhelm I and the French ambassador to Prussia took place in the resort city of Ems in western Germany. There, the German emperor and the French ambassador diplomatically and politely discussed the issue. At the end of their talks, they agreed to disagree, and while the issue was not settled, it appeared that, at least for a time, war had been averted, which was not what Bismarck wanted.

Bismarck realized that the time was right for a war with France, the last nation in Europe that could stand in the way of a united Germany. As it was, the French felt threatened by Prussian growth in the wars of the 1860s, and if the remaining southern and western German states became part of Prussia, the Prussians would not only become that much stronger but also much of its territory would border France. For both international reasons and reasons of domestic politics, Napoleon III could not allow that to happen.

Bismarck received a dispatch telegram from the Kaiser relating the events of his meeting with the French ambassador. For a moment, it seemed like there was nothing further that Bismarck could do—until he realized that he could "edit" the telegram to make it seem as if the Prussian monarch had deliberately and greatly insulted the French ambassador.

Essentially, the telegram stated that the German Kaiser would not see the French ambassador again and that he was done talking to him. In the language of diplomacy, this is almost a literal slap in the face. Making matters worse, the French agency responsible for translating the telegram confused two very similar looking words, and instead of the German officer, who was an aide to the Kaiser, delivering the message, the translator made it seem as if the message from the Prussians had been delivered by a common, lowly sergeant. This was both an insult and an indication that the Prussians had no respect for the French and their ruler.

Bismarck knew it was just a matter of hours before the Ems Dispatch, as it is known, was published in every newspaper in France. When that happened, he was sure the population would scream for war against the Prussians and that Napoleon III, looking for "glory" as his popularity wanted, would oblige them. Of course, people and officials in Prussia read about the French reaction and called for war themselves, which was exactly what Bismarck hoped would happen.

Illustration 4: Contemporary engraving of Parisians calling for war with Prussia, 1870

France mobilized its army on July 15th, 1870, declared war on the 16th, and sent its declaration to Berlin on the 19th. The states of the North German Confederation, led by Prussia, mobilized their army more rapidly than the French due to their organizational strength and the miles of railway now crisscrossing most of Germany. Additionally, the states of south Germany (the powerful state of Bavaria, along with Baden and Württemberg) declared war on France as well; apparently, the feeling for their brother Germans ran strong despite them having been loyal to Austria only recently. Bismarck, having intentionally whispered in the ears of the south German press about Napoleon's demand for German territory at their 1866 Biarritz meeting, also inflamed the anti-French feeling in the German states.

Though it did not know it, France was beaten almost before the war began. Though French soldiers actually possessed better rifles (the Chassepot) with a longer range than the Prussian Dreyse needle-gun and possessed small numbers of an early machine gun, the French Army had anticipated fighting a defensive war, hoping to break Prussian attacks on trench-works backed by artillery. On the other side, the Prussians constantly drilled for an offensive and fluid war, learning to take advantage of conditions they met on the field and not what they anticipated.

Making matters worse, most of the French artillery were bronze breech-loading cannons, which gave out quicker and were slower to load than the Prussian steel breech-loading cannons they had mass-produced in the years since the Austrian war. Though there were large-caliber Prussian guns with which to shell strong French positions, much of the Prussian artillery was smaller and mobile, allowing the Prussians to use their guns as a kind of tank without the armor. They quickly maneuvered their artillery where it was needed to support Prussian troops' breakthroughs and nullify the longer range of the French rifles.

Under much of Louis-Napoleon's reign, the French Army had been a standing army, with about 425,000 men. The French draft system was fraught with problems, the biggest one being an excessively long time of service (seven years), which both hurt the French economy and sapped soldiers' morale. When the French saw the rapidity with which Prussia defeated Austria and how effective their conscription system had been, they began to implement changes, but these were incomplete by the time of the war in 1870. At the height of the war, the number of French soldiers in the field (combat troops) was far less than the Prussians; there were approximately 950,000 Prussians compared to just over 700,000 French.

Beyond that, the French Army had very few plans and very little coordination between army groups and commanders. They, like the Austrians four years earlier, also had far fewer telegraph lines with which to quickly communicate to their headquarters and capital.

The war was a bloody and savage affair, and it lasted a relatively short time—just over six months. In that time, 45,000 Germans/Prussians and nearly 140,000 Frenchmen lost their lives. Though there were quite a few battles fought, the most important one, and the one that ultimately defeated France and brought down Napoleon III, was the Battle of Sedan.

By September, the important French fortress border town of Metz was under siege, and Napoleon III and his leading generals were determined to relieve it. The French felt that if Metz fell, the bulk of the Prusso-German armies would come pouring into western France. Never mind that German forces had already penetrated France to the north in a maneuver foreshadowing their attack in 1914.

The Germans intercepted French signals, and the two armies engaged in a series of hard-fought battles before the French realized that their attempt to relieve Metz was doomed to failure. In order to save what was left of the French Army in northwestern France, French General Patrice de MacMahon moved the army to the border town of Sedan, about one hundred miles north of Metz. When they got there, the French Army found a town in panic and the people wanting the army to leave lest their city be flattened by the Germans. The situation was so bad that a number of French troops were trampled to death in a panic to get inside the city's fortified walls. It was clear within a day that the situation for the French, many of whom were trapped outside the city in woefully unprepared positions, was hopeless.

Illustration 5: German armies are marked in dark blue, French in light blue, with the unaffected zone marked in the north.

Among those inside the walls of Sedan was Napoleon III. Both he and his generals realized that the only way out alive, both for them and the city's populace, was surrender, and this is what happened on September 2nd, 1870, when a very sick Napoleon III rode to meet with Kaiser Wilhelm I and gave up.

However, the city and the bulk of the French Army saw this move as cowardly. Napoleon's government fell, and the Third French Republic took its place (you can read more about this in Captivating History's *History of France*). The leaders of the Third Republic ordered the remaining French armies to fight on, which they did, but they were forced back to Paris by September 19th.

For four months, the Prussians and their south German allies besieged Paris, causing mass hunger (the elephants in the zoo were infamously killed for food), panic, and a brief socialist revolution (the Paris Commune, which was put down harshly by French troops when the war ended).

Eventually, with their beautiful city being shelled more and more each day and the Prussian front lines approaching, the French asked for an armistice as a preliminary to peace talks on January 26th, 1871. Though fighting went on in places for some time after, the war was essentially over.

The talks took place at the Palace of Versailles, which had been occupied by the Prussians in an additional humiliation to French pride, and the French agreed to pay an indemnity and, far more importantly, cede the French provinces of Alsace and Lorraine to a newly united German nation, for the southern states of Bavaria, Baden, and Württemberg had agreed to place themselves in a larger German state with the Prussian Kaiser as its ruler. Bavaria, due to its size, power, and independent streak, negotiated a unique agreement within the German Empire, allowing it greater autonomy within Germany.

Alsace and Lorraine had been fought over for centuries, and they contained a roughly equal number of French and German speakers. Naturally, the French residents were unhappy, and many French families left the territories.

The loss of Alsace-Lorraine was the ultimate humiliation for the French, and what's more, it made defending French territory even more difficult in the future. Politically, a whole movement arose within France known as revanchism ("revenge-ism"), which was dedicated to the reconquest of these provinces and a direct contribution to World War I.

But for Germany, a new era had begun. The German states had never been united in one entity before, and a new European power had been born. What's more, this new power had shown to the world the dominance of its armed forces and its harnessing of technology. The changes that came from the Franco-Prussian War were immense. Nations began forming general staffs for the constant upkeep and modernization of their armies. Conscription systems modeled after the Prussians were put in place throughout

Europe. Camouflage as a military science, which was born in Germany, was given priority, as was much else.

For Otto von Bismarck, the unification of Germany was the high-water mark of his career, which would last until the new Kaiser, Wilhelm II, the grandson of Wilhelm I, dismissed him in 1888 to run the state himself.

Illustration 6: This painting by Anton von Werner was done years after the end of the war. The original displeased the Kaiser, who had it destroyed. In this painting, the Kaiser (on the dais) and Bismarck (the central figure in white) are shown as they appeared in 1881, not 1871. The painting is entitled The Proclamation of the German Empire.

Chapter 3 – Wilhelm's Germany

When Wilhelm II became Kaiser in 1888, he inherited a new world power. In many ways, Germany was envied: it was powerful, innovative, and cultured. It was also feared; after all, it had won three major wars in twenty years, and it was suddenly the most populous state in Europe and the most advanced on the Continent (only England surpassed it in economic terms). It was also no secret that the young new Kaiser was determined to raise his country to new heights, which would likely come at the expense of others in Europe.

Before we delve into the complex personality of Kaiser Wilhelm II, let's take a moment to discuss life in Germany under Bismarck and the first years of the Kaiser's rule.

Firstly, despite some truly deep divisions within German society, almost every German citizen was exceedingly proud of their new country. After all, Germany had seemingly done the impossible against a great many enemies, and it was now the leading industrial power in Europe. Most, though not all, Germans were loyal to their emperor, and they worshiped Bismarck almost as a god for what he had accomplished. The army, especially the officers, claimed another place in the hearts and minds of most Germans.

Since the time of Frederick the Great, the Prussian Army had been one of the main pillars of Prussian society. Now, it was one of the main pillars of German society. Without a very effective army, Bismarck's plans would have come to naught. Though the esteem in which soldiers were held varied by region, it is safe to say that in most of Germany, officers (especially generals) were held in a sort of semi-deification. Even in retirement, most men wore the symbols of their regiment on their lapels with pride or stuffed themselves into their once perfectly fitting uniforms for national or local holidays and events. Officers would be called by their title, sometimes even by members of their families, until the day they died. For many young men in the middle and upper classes, being an officer (especially a career officer) was the highest aspiration of their lives, and if it wasn't his hope, then it was the hope of his family.

In small towns and villages throughout Germany (at the turn of the century, most Germans still lived in small towns and villages, though it was rapidly changing), the mayor usually had some military background. Many times, however, it was the highest-ranking officer, who was usually retired, in the area that was approached for the solution to a problem.

At the top of the German political food chain was the new Kaiser, Wilhelm II. His father, Frederick III, had ruled for only ninety-nine days, having known he was dying from cancer of the larynx before he took the throne. When he passed on June 15th, 1888, his son Wilhelm ascended to rule the world's newest power.

There were many in the upper class and even in his own family, the Hohenzollerns, that had trepidations about Wilhelm being Kaiser (now is a good a time as any to explain that the German word "Kaiser" is a translation of the Latin word "Caesar"). Firstly, in a time when people had very little understanding of or tolerance for physical handicaps, Wilhelm was born with a withered left arm, caused by inept obstetricians attempting to save the baby, who was a breech birth. This was made worse by the protocol of the time, which dictated that instead of being nude at least from the waist down, Wilhelm's mother, Victoria (the eldest child of the illustrious Queen Victoria of Britain), had on a long gown, under which the doctors were forced to work for reasons of "modesty." They used forceps to grip the baby's neck and shoulder, forcibly pulling him out of the womb. When the child was delivered in January 1859, he was blue and only revived by vigorous rubbing and handling. Many believe that this relatively prolonged period of oxygen deprivation at birth may have caused personality and mental issues later in life, for the Kaiser became known for being notoriously unstable when it came to his mood.

To have the future king of Prussia be physically challenged (and make no mistake, the word used, even by the emperor, was "crippled") was anathema to the Prussian aristocracy and the royal family. All the modern methods were applied, including vigorous massages on a regular basis, but nothing seemed to work. So, starting from when the future king was about six months old, other methods were used, and so-called experts from around Europe were brought in to attempt to straighten and strengthen Wilhelm's withered arm and hand, which was essentially misshapen into a claw-like appendage.

Cold seawater compresses and sprays were used. At four, the young boy was essentially stretched on a rack, a la the Dark Ages. As he approached puberty, his head and neck began to tilt to the left, but an operation cutting strained tendons stopped that. Other weird methods were also tried. The boy was forced to place his arm in the abdomen of freshly killed deer, the thinking being that somehow the heat and blood might help. Of course, it did not. When told of this, Queen Victoria called it "revolting and idiotic." Other techniques included shock therapy to the arm and tying his good arm to his body to force the prince to use the withered one (he couldn't).

Historians over the years have placed varying levels of importance on the effect of all of this (both the deformity and the treatments) on the Kaiser's personality. While it's a stretch to blame all of the Kaiser's actions on his arm, it also must have had some effect, especially during a time of such intolerance.

What did happen was that the Kaiser developed an extraordinarily strong right hand and arm, which he would use to impress or overawe certain people when shaking hands. He also developed quite a shot and loved hunting, though the game had to be driven in his direction and the weapon primed for him. In his elder years, when he was in exile in Holland, he chopped large amounts of wood with his one arm and could frequently outpace others with two good arms. He also developed into quite an able horseman.

Still, whether it was an effect of the torturous methods he was forced to undergo as a child, the simple fact that he was "deformed," or perhaps just his personality, Kaiser Wilhelm II turned into a mercurial ruler with an inferiority complex. He was determined to outshine his royal relatives in England and Russia (King George V and Tsar Nicholas II of Russia) and other lesser nobility, and he was never hesitant to brag, threaten, or coerce others to get his way. He was a notorious practical joker, but had he not been emperor, he likely would have gotten punched in the mouth, for many of his "jokes" came at the public or physical expense of others, usually those in high places in the army, navy, or government.

Wilhelm and the House of Hohenzollern went to great lengths to hide his arm. In both stills and moving pictures, as well as in person, he would hold a pair of white gloves in his left arm, making it appear longer or of normal length. At times of official business, when he wore a full military uniform, his left hand would clasp the hilt of a sword or he would hold his left hand in his right to attempt to downplay the handicap.

Illustration 7: Kaiser Wilhelm II during WWI

Illustration 8: The ex-Kaiser in Dutch exile

When Wilhelm became Kaiser in 1888, he was determined to rule directly. He chafed under both the counsel of and the legend of Otto von Bismarck, and he knew that as long as the "Iron Chancellor" remained in office, he would be overshadowed. On March 20th, 1890, a little over a year and a half after taking the throne, Wilhelm felt strong enough politically to fire the man who had created a united Germany.

Bismarck did not go happily, but he had no choice. To his friends and trusted journalists, he told them his worries about Germany's future under Wilhelm, whom he believed was unstable and would drag Germany into a war it could not win.

Bismarck is famous for uniting Germany, and statues of the man are still found throughout Germany, as are street names and schools. However, in domestic politics, Bismarck was not as successful or popular. One of his most infamous policies was called *Der Kulturkampf* ("the culture struggle"). This was aimed at the Catholics, who made up a very sizable minority in the country and a majority in the new states of southern and southwestern Germany. Virtually all Prussians were Lutheran, as was most of the north German population. The Thirty Years' War (1618-1648), a religious war between Catholics and Protestants within Europe, was fought mainly in Germany. Millions died, and old prejudices were still very much alive during the time of Bismarck.

Bismarck and other Protestants in the ruling classes in northern Germany were suspicious of the Catholics in the south, mostly for one main reason: they suspected that the Catholics would be more loyal to the pope in Rome than to the Kaiser in Berlin. To limit that perceived loyalty and to further German unity (at least in Bismarck's eyes), he began to put forward a series of sanctions and regulations on the Catholic Church and its clergy in 1871. This continued until 1875; by then, Bismarck had realized his policies were a miscalculation and had caused further division in the country.

Most of these policies put Catholic clergy, education, and hospitals under government control. For example, the clergy had to be approved by the state, universities and other religious schools were subject to inspection (theoretically, this meant Protestant schools as well, but everyone knew it was the Catholics who were being targeted), and marriage became a civil ceremony. Tensions got so bad that a Catholic zealot came close to assassinating

Bismarck in 1874. Liberals in the country decried the discriminatory policies, and the Catholic Centre Party gained a significant number of seats in the German parliament, effectively stymieing Bismarck's policies and forcing the rollback of many.

In the late 19th and early 20th centuries, the winds of change were blowing over Western Europe, mostly brought on by the Industrial Revolution, which was reaching new heights in cities throughout the western part of the Continent but slowly moving eastward as well.

The list of changes that took place is profound. The population was moving in large numbers from the countryside and villages to the cities, changing both the economies and cultures of both. Rapid growth in the city meant housing shortages but also tremendous amounts of building projects (including roads, rails, subways, and bridges). The crowded conditions brought about epidemics, sometimes on a huge scale, forcing politicians, doctors, and city planners to come up with solutions for problems that had never really been faced before.

In the workplace, which meant factories, people who had never been outside of their hometowns or districts except *maybe* more than once or twice in their lives were now living and working with people who might as well have been foreigners. Dialects prevalent all over Europe changed rapidly into new urban ones. Food, dress, and much else were new and changed over time, especially among the middle classes.

Though many people from countries began an immense wave of emigration to the United States (which brought about its own problems, both in America and Europe), millions remained. People speak of America as a "melting pot" of cultures, but the same thing happened in cities in Europe and Germany in the late 19th and early 20th centuries.

For people from Berlin, Bavarians might as well have been from another country (until 1871, they were) and vice versa. The same thing went on all over Europe, as people from rural areas moved into cities. Of course, in larger cities near the borders, there were more than just new arrivals from other provinces. There were also people from other countries. Some of them had been in these cities for years, while others were newcomers. This, of course, brought on new and larger problems of language, religion, and beliefs. For the most part, people managed to get by, and there were few large issues. However, underneath everything, age-old prejudices were brewing. Sometimes they rose to the top and made headlines or rumors, but these were usually temporary or tamped down by the authorities.

Of course, we're speaking here of anti-Semitism. More will follow on the topic, but for now, suffice it to say that Germany's Jewish population, which had existed in the country for centuries, was now being exposed to old hatreds magnified by the concentration of newcomers. These newcomers were oftentimes poor, rural, ill-educated, and brought up with prejudices against people they had never really known, for most of Germany's and Europe's Jews lived in the cities.

In Vienna, Austria, a frustrated young artist from the small city of Linz, whose family doctor was Jewish and who had a Jewish friend help him sell his watercolor postcards, was overawed by the cosmopolitan nature of the Austrian capital, which, in many ways, was experiencing the same changes as in Berlin. Not helping matters was the anti-Semitism of Vienna's mayor, Karl Lueger, who frequently blamed the city's ills on the Jews. Initially, he was put off by the vulgarity of the anti-Semitic press in Vienna, but as he was exposed to it more and more, his outlook began to change. This young man later recorded his experiences in a book:

Once, as I was strolling through the inner city, I suddenly encountered an apparition in a black caftan and black hair locks. Is this a Jew? was my first thought...For, to be sure, they had not looked like that in Linz. I observed the man furtively and cautiously, but the longer I stared at this foreign face, scrutinizing feature for feature, the more my first question assumed a new form: is this a German? ...the more I saw, the more sharply they became distinguished in my eyes from the rest of humanity...For me this was the time of the greatest spiritual upheaval I have ever had to go through. I had ceased to be a weak-kneed cosmopolitan and become an anti-Semite.

As I am sure you have guessed, the young man was Adolf Hitler, and he was not alone in his feelings, which drew adherents as more changes and the later economic depression occurred.

Factory work was dangerous. It still is, but at a time when the first truly gigantic factory complexes were being built, health and safety issues were decidedly lower on the list of things factory owners and governments had to deal with. That soon changed. Faced with the immediate danger of the new factories and the mines that fed them, as well as the health issues that followed and with the crowded living conditions created by the new economy, workers began to organize.

As you may know, by the late 1800s, many of these workers were espousing the new theory of communism and its less militant cousin, socialism. Communism, which was put forward by German thinkers Karl Marx and Friedrich Engels (mostly working in England), states that economics functioned in a similar way as the newly popular theory of evolution put forward by Charles Darwin. In communist theory, human economic activity moved from a feudal/medieval stage slowly into one based on profit, localized in small towns and villages while evolving into an economy focused on factories and capitalism. According to Marx and Engels, throughout history, the rich and powerful have exploited the poor, with this only getting worse as time goes by. With the advent of industrial capitalism, they believed conditions would grow so unequal that eventually, the workers would have no choice but to overthrow the upper classes and form a "worker's state" in which all property would be communally held—thus, the name of "communism." Of course, this is a very simple explanation, but even this short explanation, put in a pamphlet with compelling statistics, personal stories, and illustrations, was enough to move many of the workers in European cities toward communism or socialism.

Socialism and communism are not necessarily the same thing, though the words have been and are constantly used interchangeably. In Germany and elsewhere, a less militant socialist movement sprang up in response to the changes brought about by the Industrial Revolution. This was social democracy, and in Germany, the party representing these ideas was the SPD (for *Sozialdemokratische Partei Deutschlands* or "Social Democratic Party of Germany").

An adequate and succinct definition of European social democratic beliefs in the 19th and 20th centuries comes from Washington State University Professor Paul Brians, who in comparing social democratic ideas in 19th-century America with European ones, said, "Social democrats were more successful in Europe, particularly in Scandinavia, following a gradualist approach which involved high taxes to enforce relative economic equality, government regulation of industry, nationalization of large industries, and social welfare."

In the years before Bismarck's forced retirement, the Social Democrats became the largest party in Germany. Though Bismarck believed that socialism (and its more militant corollary, communism) was harmful to both the economy and the existing social structure and spent years enacting oppressive laws against it, he also realized that without some change in the workplace, violent disruption was likely. To that end, Bismarck, working with leading

Social Democrats who hated the Iron Chancellor, developed some of the most forward-thinking social welfare laws in the world. Work hours were reduced, the workweek decreased, socialized medicine was put in place, workplace safety standards began, and changes to housing and housing laws were enacted and evolved, though the poorer districts of any German city at the time were unsafe, crowded, and unhealthy places to live. In many ways, Germany, which had an almost completely absolute monarchy after 1890, was the most progressive industrial state in the world, and this was only after just twenty or so years of being a nation.

Germany and the World before WWI

Germans of all stripes could be rightly proud of the accomplishments they had achieved since 1871. Only one thing remained: "a place in the sun." This phrase, attributed to Kaiser Wilhelm II, was actually first uttered by his foreign minister, Bernhard von Bülow, in 1897. Speaking in a debate in the Reichstag about foreign policy, von Bülow said, "We wish to throw no one into the shade, but we also demand our own place in the sun." This statement referred to Germany's wish to participate in the second great age of imperialism, which took place in the latter part of the 19th and early 20th centuries.

For many reasons—economic, political, military, and religious— the great powers of Europe and the United States began to carve up the world between them, conquering many of the territories, kingdoms, and ancient states of Asia, Africa, and the Pacific. The leaders in this "race" were Great Britain and France, although Belgium, Italy, Holland, and Russia all took part. Japan was also a participant in Asia, having developed a modern economy in an amazing amount of time between 1870 and the late 1890s.

As we have seen, Germany had been divided into many states before 1864, and while the Germans were busy fighting for unification and then attempting to build a nation, the other powers of Europe were busy conquering much of the world. This was why von Bülow and the Kaiser wanted "a place in the sun" for Germany, which meant one thing—an empire.

Though there were a great many factors contributing to European and especially German imperialism in the 1890s onward, the desire for "a place in the sun" fit in perfectly with Kaiser Wilhelm's upbringing and personality. Here he was, a "cripple," now in command of one of the world's greatest armies and economies. This was his chance to show that he and Germany were strong, dominant, and second to none.

To do this, the Kaiser, who was an avid sailor and who attended the famed sailing regatta at Cowes in England every year (along with his many royal cousins, who frequently and sometimes openly derided his appearance), was determined to build a navy to compete with and eventually outnumber the greatest navy in the history of the world to that time, the Royal Navy of Great Britain.

Illustration 9: In this turn-of-the-century cartoon, the nations of Europe (Great Britain, Germany, Russia, and France), along with Japan, contemplate the division of a protesting China. Note the aggressive attitude of the Kaiser toward his grandmother Victoria, the symbol of Great Britain.

Building a navy capable of challenging the Royal Navy was a daunting if not impossible task for Wilhelm's Germany. At the outbreak of WWI, the Royal Navy consisted of 82 battleships, 136 cruisers, 142 destroyers, 80 torpedo boats, 80 submarines, and 15 early versions of aircraft carriers. The navy also included over 300 support and other vessels (riverine patrol boats, oilers, supply ships, etc.), and during the war, the Americans (as it did in WWII) lent or gave the British another nearly 500 ships of varying kinds (excluding major combat ships, such as battleships and cruisers).

At the beginning of the 20th century, when Wilhelm decided to build his navy (*Kriegsmarine* in German), these numbers were a bit smaller, but the strength of the Royal Navy still far exceeded any other nation. Actually, British policy was (and had been for some time) that the Royal Navy would be half again as strong as the next *two* greatest navies in the world. Britain's commercial life depended on the Royal Navy's protection, either in actuality (escort merchant ships) or as a deterrent. More importantly, the Royal Navy (whose "Home Fleet," based in northern Scotland, was its largest) kept the United Kingdom safe from invasions. The survival of their nation and their empire depended on the Royal Navy.

Until this point in time, German foreign policy, for the most part, had been astute and well-thought-out. That was due almost exclusively to Bismarck. The Iron Chancellor also realized that Germany was a "saturated power." By this, he meant that Germany would not actively seek out additional territory in Europe or elsewhere. He knew that the chances of war would greatly increase if Germany attempted to increase the size of its empire, realizing that the great powers of Europe were already wary of his nation, having come so far and so fast. By the time Bismarck was pushed out of office by the Kaiser, the German Army was the strongest in Europe, and its economy was second to only that of Great Britain— and all of that in roughly thirty years' time.

Bismarck, like most other statesmen of the time, knew that for centuries the British had been guided by their policy of trying to maintain a "balance of power" in Europe. Simply put, with no one country or bloc of countries dominating the others, the chances of war and threats to Britain's economy were lessened.

When Bismarck left, Germany's foreign policy changed radically, as you have read. Surprisingly, while the Germans were eager to construct a fleet that would be a "deterrent fleet" (in the words of the Reich secretary of the navy, Admiral Alfred von Tirpitz, whose last name you might recognize from the famous

WWII battleship that was named in his honor), they believed that common sense and the new balance of power in Europe should make England a German ally.

The Germans believed that Britain's economic, imperial, and historic rivalries with France and Russia, the other two great powers of Europe, made it a natural ally of Germany. To an extent, this was true, even down to the German roots of the English royal family, and had this been the only factor the English considered, Germany and Great Britain might have indeed found themselves allies at the beginning of the 20th century. However, a number of German miscalculations made that an impossibility.

The Kaiser's shrill behavior and speeches put the English on alert, offended English sensibilities, and challenged its historic role as the middle-man/peacemaker between the powers of Europe and, to a degree, the world. On the twenty-fifth anniversary of the founding of a united Germany in 1896, Wilhelm, playing to his own vanity and the patriotic feelings of his subjects on that important day, announced that, from that point forward, Germany would demand to be consulted in all European affairs and all important world affairs. As you might imagine, that rubbed British sensibilities quite the wrong way. The other powers of the world were not exactly thrilled either.

However, the German argument did make sense, and many in Britain believed that the balance of power could be kept with German and British interests aligned. The Germans had calculated quite well in that regard, as the balance of power was one of the pillars of British foreign policy and power, but it was not the only one.

The British could be challenged commercially. After all, the economy of the world at that time was based on economic competition and free enterprise. The British could also make room at the diplomatic table for the Germans: after all, they were a great power and had to be taken into consideration. But the one thing the

British absolutely could not tolerate was a naval rival, and it was clear from both the Kaiser's public and private utterings that he meant that Germany's "deterrent fleet" would be aimed at only one power: Great Britain. What's more, as time went by and the world entered the 20th century, Wilhelm's words and actions made it clear that he was intent on building a German navy that was not just a deterrent to the Royal Navy but superior to it. This pushed Britain right into the arms of France and Russia, two powers with which it had relatively recently been at war.

Of course, Germany could not hope to build a navy to rival Britain's in a short time. The plan set out by von Tirpitz would take twenty-five years. It was a pipe dream from the beginning. It assumed that the British would not match or out-do Germany's naval growth to maintain her dominance at sea (which she did), presumed smooth economic times were ahead, and, strangely of all, was proposed to not cost any extra money at all, the idea being that taxes and other revenues of Germany's rapidly growing economy would pay for it without the government having to borrow the money or run up a deficit. Of course, this did not happen, and by the time World War One began, Germany had already begun to go into debt to pay for its military.

Germany's "place in the sun" would eventually amount to...well, not much. By the time that Wilhelm sent the navy (along with accompanying expeditionary forces) out to claim that place, there really wasn't that much left unclaimed. By August 1914, the German Empire consisted of the city and bay of Jiaozhou in China (then known as Kiaochow by the Europeans); the Marshall Islands and the newly named Bismarck Archipelago (a group of islands off the coast of Papua New Guinea) in the Pacific and Cameroon; Togo, Namibia (then known as German Southwest Africa), and Tanzania (then called German East Africa) in Africa.

And what did Germany get from these colonies? Nothing for the most part, except some poorly located ports, and it ended up costing Germany more to keep these colonies than any benefit it received. Additionally, the seizure of these areas and Germany's crowing about it for German domestic political consumption did nothing but annoy and alarm the other colonial powers of Europe, along with the United States and, to a lesser degree, Japan, both of which had significant imperial possessions in the Pacific region.

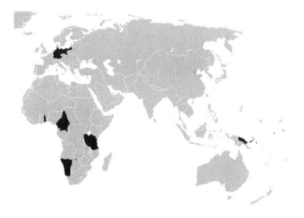

Illustration 10: German Empire before WWI

As you can see from the map above, Germany's colonies were not only few (comparatively) but also separated by considerable distances over land and water. Both France and Great Britain had the location and/or the naval resources to either involve their imperial possessions in their respective economies or connect them by rail (in the case of Britain in Africa). The Germans were not able to use British railways, and their naval resources were stretched thin trying to supply and protect their empire.

One of the "blessings" for the native peoples of the German Empire was that, generally speaking, as long as they did not attack or harass German troops, officials, or citizens, they were left alone. Yes, their resources were exploited, but none of the territories that you see was very rich in the first place, and even before the Germans arrived, they did not have advanced economies and trade to other areas. Namibia was almost 100 percent desert. German East Africa and German Cameroon (Tanzania and Cameroon) were verdant but harsh and not the richest of areas resource-wise. The same was true for Togo, the German part of Papua New Guinea, and the other German islands in the Pacific.

Papua New Guinea provides an interesting example of the German government. While the British struggled with the tribes of New Guinea in the land under their control, for the most part, the Germans did not. This came down to two related reasons: religion and cannibalism.

Many of the tribes of Papua New Guinea at the time (and until the first decades of the last half of the 20th century) practiced cannibalism. Most of this had to do with religious/spiritual rites and how they related to war or combat. The British, and later the Australians, sent missionaries to both convert the native populations, which consisted of many disparate tribes or clans, to Christianity and end cannibalism. In many of these cases, at least initially, this resulted in bloodshed and repression, and sometimes the missionaries were served for dinner. This provoked another harsh backlash.

The Germans were content to let the natives, who were ostensibly under their control, continue as they had for millennia, as long as the Germans were left alone. This made the German part of Papua New Guinea relatively peaceful during the time Wilhelm II controlled the area. To begin a war with the natives would mean additional costs in lives, manpower, and supplies, which would have to be brought in from the other side of the globe.

In China, however, German behavior was marked for its disregard for life. From 1899 to 1901, the Society of Righteous Harmonious Fists united millions of Chinese peasants together in what is known in the West as the Boxer Rebellion. The Boxer Rebellion cost millions of lives, and it was the result of a conflict with the European powers, which claimed "concessions" in Chinese cities that gave them not only preferential trading rights but also allowed the Europeans (along with the Japanese and, to a lesser extent, the Americans) to apply their own legal systems and much else. Naturally, this caused much resentment among the Chinese, who were treated as second-class citizens in their own countries in the areas under foreign control.

Illustration 11: Troops of the Eight-Nation Alliance in China, 1900. Left to right: Britain, United States, Australia, British India, Germany, France, Austria-Hungary, Italy, and Japan.

In Beijing, the anti-foreign, anti-Christian Boxers surrounded and besieged the Legation Quarter, where the imperial powers had their embassies, most of their residences, and churches, along with much else. The foreigners eventually broke the siege in Beijing as well as the uprisings elsewhere (as a side note, the Chinese government, which was criticized for being weak and "allowing" the foreigners in the country in the first place, tacitly encouraged the Boxers until the tide turned). The Japanese and Germans, in particular, behaved brutally in response to Chinese attacks, which, it must be admitted, sometimes crossed the line into atrocities. It was in China that the Germans picked up one of their WWI/WWII nicknames after Kaiser Wilhelm gave a speech to his departing troops at Bremerhaven in 1900:

No quarter will be given, no prisoners will be taken. Let all who fall into your hands be at your mercy. Just as the Huns a thousand years ago, under the leadership of Attila, gained a reputation in virtue of which they still live in historical tradition, so may the name of Germany become known in such a manner in China that no Chinaman will ever again dare to look askance at a German.

Even during a time of war and intense racism, Wilhelm's speech and the behavior of his men in China caught the world's attention. From then on, the Germans were often referred to as "Huns."

On the other side of the world, the Kaiser's brash and off-putting behavior and speeches caused the other great powers of Europe (with the exception of Austria-Hungary) to improve their relationships with each other and, in some cases, form official alliances.

In Morocco, in two crises separated by six years (1905 and 1911), the Kaiser attempted to drive a wedge between France and Great Britain, which had signed the Entente Cordiale in 1904. Part of this agreement between the two nations stipulated that England and France would each control one of the two remaining independent territories of Africa (excluding Liberia, a nation developed by freed American enslaved peoples, which had the support and backing of the US). These two territories were Egypt, which the British coveted, and Morocco, which the French desired.

When the French made their move on Morocco in 1905, Wilhelm visited the region and announced that he believed that Morocco was a free and sovereign nation and that he would only deal with the sultan of Morocco. This was obviously hypocritical given Germany's own colonies, but Wilhelm hoped that the French would be dissuaded in Morocco and perhaps seek territory elsewhere, perhaps at the expense of England.

Wilhelm could not have been more wrong. His interference actually drove the French and English closer together. They, along with Spain, which was directly across the Strait of Gibraltar from Morocco, convened a conference to decide the fate of Morocco without the Kaiser's input. In a short time, the French and Spanish (helped by the English) divided most of Morocco between them. It did not matter if the Kaiser would only deal with the sultan now, as he was just a figurehead.

In 1911, there were several Moroccan uprisings against the sultan, who was and who was seen as a French puppet. In Fez, which was ostensibly governed directly by the sultan, a violent uprising against the ruler began. To retain control, Sultan Abd al-Hafid asked for French troops. The French used this opportunity to take control of the remaining "free" part of Morocco, which the Kaiser saw as a direct affront to him, as he had both friendly relations with the sultan and had recognized him as the legitimate ruler of the country. In response to French action, Wilhelm sent the SMS *Panther* to the Moroccan harbor of Agadir, hoping to encourage the uprising against France.

In accord with the Entente Cordiale, Britain announced its support for France, as did Russia, which had its own agreement with Paris. Germany's ally in Europe, Austria-Hungary, remained silent on the matter, and, isolated, Wilhelm was forced to back down.

This second Moroccan crisis caused a great deal of resentment in Germany, and it again drove Britain and France closer together. The two powers concluded a naval treaty shortly after the crisis, which led to a mutual defense pact that eventually included Russia. Wilhelm had isolated Germany and set the alliances of WWI in ever-hardening cement.

Chapter 4 – The Great War

Very few people were surprised when Europe found itself at war in 1914. Since the French defeat by Prussia/Germany in 1871, international events seemed to be inexorably headed in that direction. The French wanted revenge. The large nations of Europe and a couple of smaller ones competed for an empire around the world. The economies of Great Britain, France, and Germany (and, to a lesser degree, Russia and Italy) were growing almost exponentially as the first years of the 20th century went by, causing another type of competition. There was an arms race at sea between England and Germany, and on land, the powers were developing new and more deadly weapons to equip their growing armies.

In southeastern Europe, the decline of the Ottoman Empire meant that the peoples of the Balkans, most of them under Turkish control for centuries, were both asserting their independence and struggling for influence and/or territory in the area themselves. In addition to the smaller territories of the region, Austria-Hungary sought to expand its power and control. Since it was an essentially land-locked empire, it was shut out of the race for overseas territories that consumed the British, French, Russians, Italians, and Belgians (who controlled the giant territory of the Congo in southern-central Africa).

Illustration 12: The alliances of Europe, 1914–1915

The rule of the Ottomans had, for the most part, kept a lid on the ethnic and religious hatred that existed in the Balkans for centuries. For much of their rule (from the 16th century onward), their iron-fisted control and power kept the peoples of the Balkan Peninsula from going at each other's throats. There was also the matter of those people hating the Turks and their religion more than they hated each other.

From 1912 to 1913, the Serbs, Bulgarians, and Greeks attacked the weakened Turkish imperial forces in the Balkans and pushed them out of almost all of Europe, except for a small part of Greece and some Greek islands off the Turkish coast (the Turks' empire would be further reduced when it fell apart at the end of the First World War). This was the First Balkan War.

With the Turks out of the way, for the most part, these three countries then turned on each other in the short Second Balkan War, which lasted through much of 1913. In this war, the Bulgarians attacked the Serbs and Greeks, attempting to carve out a small empire of their own. It did not work, and the Serbs and Greeks pushed the Bulgarians back into their own country before the Bulgars sued for peace.

What concerns us here is that at the end of the Second Balkan War, the Kingdom of Serbia doubled in size. The area annexed by the Serbs was populated by a Serb majority, but with the growth of their nation and their armed forces, the Serbs (ruled by King Peter I and the military) were eager to expand their territory into areas populated by a Serb majority or sizable minority. These were the territories of Montenegro and Bosnia-Herzegovina.

The problem was that neither of these territories wanted to be part of Serbia. They knew from the rhetoric coming from Belgrade (the Serbs' capital) that life under Serbian rule was likely not going to be much or any better than what they had experienced under the Ottomans.

Enter the other major player in the region: the Austro-Hungarian Empire. The Austro-Hungarians were essentially locked out of the "second age of imperialism" that occurred in the 19th and early 20th centuries. Though they were not a completely land-locked power, the Austro-Hungarian Imperial Navy was not a force able to sustain and defend overseas colonies, so they looked with keen eyes at the power vacuum in the Balkans in the hope of gaining the prestige and resources that came with adding territory.

Nothing about the Balkans is simple, and its history would have you reading and rereading the same page over and over in order to keep track of the who, what, and where of the diplomatic and military wrangling that took place in the late 19th and early 20th centuries. In 1878, at the end of yet another war between the Russians and Turks, the great powers of Europe met in Berlin to hammer out a new European settlement. For Turkey, this meant, among other things, that it would have to give up Bosnia-Herzegovina to Austria-Hungary in all but name. The Austro-Hungarians were given the right to administer and occupy the area for thirty years (no one at the peace table believed that they would leave at the end of this period).

In 1908, there was an uprising within the Ottoman government, which further weakened the empire. Concerned that this ultra-nationalist movement (known as the Young Turks) might attempt to reestablish the Ottoman Empire in Europe, the Austrian emperor ordered his army to annex Bosnia-Herzegovina directly. With that, the Austro-Hungarian Empire and the Serbians were on a collision course.

All the powers of Europe were concerned with the situation in the Balkans, but none believed that the problems there would lead to anything more than a regional war, if that. The two outside powers most concerned with the situation were Russia and Germany.

Traditionally, the Russians played the role of "big brother" to the Serbs. Both kingdoms were Eastern Orthodox. The vast majority of people within each country were Slavic. The Serbs used the Cyrillic alphabet, as did the Russians. Each nation had a unique outlook on the world but shared more of it with each other than anyone else. Russia could be expected to respond, in some way, to any direct threat to the Kingdom of Serbia. The Serbs knew this and counted on it.

For their part, the Austro-Hungarians were partners with Germany. The ruling Habsburg family were ethnically German, and the history of Germany and the German states was often intertwined with that of Austria and its rulers. However, unlike the relationship between Serbia and Russia, the Austrians and the Germans (and, before them, the Prussians) had warred with each other—more than once, in fact. Still, at a time when the Austrians were facing challenges from Italy, which coveted the eastern coast of the Adriatic Sea, and Serbia (which could and did mean Russia), the closest thing they had to a friend was Kaiser Wilhelm.

The relationship between Austrian Emperor Franz Joseph I and Kaiser Wilhelm II was not as close. Franz Joseph was many years older than Wilhelm, who was the same age as Franz Joseph's eldest son, Rudolf (who was highly popular and who, along with his beloved mistress Mary von Vetsera, committed suicide in 1889). The Austrian emperor (like almost everyone else) thought Wilhelm was unstable, brash, and a braggart, but Germany was the only nation, for reasons of both kinship and location, that Austria-Hungary could really turn to in a crisis, and Wilhelm knew it.

This was the situation in central and southeastern Europe in June 1914 when the Austrian heir to the throne, Franz Ferdinand (Rudolf's cousin and the unloved nephew of the emperor), visited Sarajevo, the capital of Bosnia-Herzegovina to tour and inspect the situation in the province of what would someday be his empire. It was also quite clear to everyone, especially the Serbs, that that archduke's visit was a show of strength and intent aimed directly at the Kingdom of Serbia as a warning not to meddle in the region.

It was already too late for that. Bosnia-Herzegovina was (and is still to a degree) populated by a variety of different ethnic groups. The three most populous were (in no particular order) the Serbs, Croats, and Bosnian Muslims. The Croatians were predominantly Catholic and traditionally looked to western and central Europe for aid, culture, and much else. Genetically, the Bosnian Muslims could've been Serbian, Croatian, or a variety of the different groups living in the area, which also included Albanians, Macedonians, and Slovenes, but during the centuries-long Ottoman occupation, they had converted to Islam. By 1914, the hatred between the groups in the area was based on religion, but by the 20th century, the Muslim Bosnians (or Bosniaks) were essentially a completely different ethnic and cultural group.

Though King Peter I of Serbia and those around him wanted to expand Serbia even at the expense of Bosnia-Herzegovina (and, therefore, Austria-Hungary), they knew that they were in no position militarily to challenge the Austrians, who were still considered a world power.

The Austrians themselves were quite aware of their real position in the world—they were a declining power. Within the Austro-Hungarian Empire, dozens of ethnicities and cultures, from large to local, vied for power, rights, and influence. Over the past forty years or so since the defeat of 1866 at the hands of the Prussians, the Hapsburg dynasty had taken a variety of steps to restore some life into what many around the world saw as a dying empire. The most obvious was the power-sharing agreement with the Hungarians and its ruling aristocracy. There were other attempts to control the situation, from granting more privileges and rights to the different minorities in the country to clamping down on them at times. By 1914, both the Habsburgs and the Hungarians were hoping that a war with the increasingly hostile Serbs would bring the country together, at least for a time.

So, on one side, the Austro-Hungarians were hoping to find an excuse to attack and absorb Serbia, and on the other hand, there were the Serbs, who were themselves eager to expand their influence, if not their borders.

The Austrians knew that unless they had a very good reason to war on Serbia, the world would condemn them as the large empire picking on their "poor, small neighbor." Thus, Emperor Franz Joseph and his hardline chief of staff, General Count Franz Conrad von Hötzendorf, could not be sure they would have the backing of their one and only ally, Germany. However, given a serious Serbian provocation, Germany might make such an exception.

Within Serbia, King Peter I and most of his generals were for expanding Serbia's boundaries but not in a military confrontation with Austria. They knew that if they went to war with Austria-Hungary, they would be defeated quickly. They hoped that a situation might appear in the future (such as serious ethnic strife or the division or fall of the Austrian Empire) of which they could take advantage through political/diplomatic means or intrigue.

Unfortunately, for the Serbs, within its army and its population (especially among the Serb minority population in Bosnia-Herzegovina) was a large and influential group of Serbian ultra-nationalists who were determined to annex Bosnia to Serbia in some way. To do this, they planned and carried out small guerrilla-style attacks and intimidation within Bosnia, but they were mostly just an annoyance to authorities.

However, this group, called "Unification or Death" (*Уједињење или смрт* / *Ujedinjenje ili smrt* in Serbo-Croatian), more popularly known by its more sinister name of the Black Hand, decided on a more radical course when it was announced that Austrian Crown Prince Archduke Franz Ferdinand would be visiting Bosnia with his pregnant wife, Sophie, in late June 1914.

The commander of the Black Hand, a Serbian colonel named Dragutin Dimitrijević, an intelligence officer in the Serbian Army who had organized an assassination and overthrow of the Serbian government in 1903, decided to take a radical step. He recruited a group of Bosnian Serbs to carry out an assassination attempt of the Austrian crown prince.

As you may know, Archduke Ferdinand and his wife were driving through Sarajevo in an open car when one of the members of the Black Hand, nineteen-year-old Gavrilo Princip, leaped on the running board of the archduke's car and emptied his pistol into the royal couple, who both died, including the unborn child Sophie was carrying. Princip was soon arrested and beaten, and he confessed. He was kept in jail throughout the war, dying of malnutrition and sickness in April 1918.

With the murder of Franz Ferdinand, Austria-Hungary had its excuse for a war, which is quite ironic since Franz Ferdinand was not a popular figure in the higher echelons of the Austrian royal family and government. He had called for more minority rights and autonomy, and he would have likely been much more open to talks with Serbia than anyone else in the ruling dynasty.

Despite his unpopularity in the ruling circles of the Austro-Hungarian leadership, Franz Ferdinand and his wife were given the elaborate send-off their positions required. Once the mourning was over, everyone expected the Austrians to make demands on Serbia.

It actually took until July 23rd for the Austrian terms to be delivered to Belgrade. The end product, a document that listed a number of things the Austrians required of the Serbian government, was actually an ultimatum. In other words, Serbia had to do all of those things or else face Austria-Hungary in a war. There were ten demands on the list, and in actuality, the Serbs were willing to comply with a couple of them. However, complying with the others would mean that Serbia would cease to be an independent state. For instance, the Austrians essentially demanded full power *within* Serbia to investigate the assassination themselves and to choose which officers and administrators would be removed from the Serbian government and army.

While waiting for the ultimatum to arrive, the Serbs consulted Russia, which replied that in the case of Austria-Hungary mobilization, the Russians would mobilize as well. With the Russian announcement, France declared that it would abide by its treaty obligations with Tsar Nicholas II and mobilize its army. On the night of July 23rd, the British offered to mediate the crisis, but in reality, their offer was both too late and was never going to be accepted anyway, for the Austrians knew the Serbians could not agree to all their demands.

Before they issued their ultimatum, though, the Austro-Hungarians had made sure they would not be headed into a crisis alone. They began talks with Kaiser Wilhelm II during the week of July 1st. The Austrians essentially knew that German support was there in case of war, but when they asked the Kaiser for his support, they used the word "punish" in reference to Serbia without explicitly saying that this punishment meant war. It did not matter. Without consulting his chancellor or his generals, the Kaiser issued what is known to history as the "blank check." Wilhelm promised to support Austria in whatever course they took, and he definitely knew that could include war, though when the Austrian invasion of Serbia did take place, it is said to have taken Wilhelm by surprise. By that time, the Serbians had issued a reply to the Austrian ultimatum in which they apologized profusely for the assassination of Franz Ferdinand (the Serbian king and those around him truly did not know what Colonel Dimitrijević had planned) while at the same time rejecting Austria's terms and offering counter-terms.

This was not the first time that Wilhelm had made a rash judgment and been surprised when the outcome didn't go his way, and it wouldn't be the last. However, he had a treaty with Austria that he could not (and would not) abrogate. He also knew that if Austria attacked Serbia, Russia would attack Austria, and a powerful Russia in central Europe was the last thing the Germans wanted. Wilhelm was also keenly aware that German public opinion was overwhelmingly pro-Austrian, and for a number of years, the German government, which was authoritarian and constructed decidedly in favor of the wealthy, especially the wealthy landowners of Prussia, had been facing calls for reform. The Kaiser hoped that this foreign policy crisis and perhaps war would unite the country behind him and the ruling elite once again.

On July 28th, after rejecting Serbia's reply, Austria-Hungary declared war on the small Balkan country. No one believed that the Serbians could hold out long against the Austrians, and Russia was not about to allow a great Austrian presence on its borders and be in control of one of its closest allies and friends. On July 30th, Russian troops on the Austrian border went on full alert. Between July 28th and August 1st, Britain, France, and Germany all tried to prevail upon Austria and Serbia to stand down to no effect, and on August 1st, the French announced the mobilization of their powerful army.

On the same day, Germany announced the mobilization of its army and declared war, in succession, on Russia, France, and Belgium, which, though aligned with France to a large degree, was a neutral nation, but as the world was about to find out, it was key to German planning.

Great Britain, in keeping with its treaty obligations with France and Russia and in keeping with its desire to maintain a balance of power in Europe, declared war on Germany on August 1st, 1914. Five days later, the Austrians declared war on Russia. With that, most of Europe was at war.

German planning and execution

The German war plans called for the rapid mobilization of both its army and navy. Knowing that the more modern French Army would mobilize more rapidly than the antiquated Russian Army, which had to concentrate its armies from great distances with few railroads, Germany planned to deploy the bulk of its forces in the west, hoping to launch a knockout blow against the French before the Russians could mount an offensive in the east and before Great Britain could get the bulk of its army to the Continent. With the French and British out of the war, the Germans could then move its western armies east to aid the Austrians against the slow-moving Russians.

As you will see on the following page, the German plan was based on early 20th-century plans developed by Field Marshal Alfred *VON* Schlieffen, and it has since become known as the Schlieffen Plan. The Germans hoped to replicate their quick victory of 1870/71 over the French, and the Schlieffen Plan essentially captured the same idea that had been used some forty years before but with the addition of attacking through neutral Belgium in the hope of surprising the French and British, who they felt would be attacking eastward along the Franco-German border. As they did, the Germans would be wheeling around behind them to cut them off from their homeland, supplies, and base of operations. The war would be over quickly—or so the Germans thought.

Illustration 13: The Schlieffen Plan, as designed between 1905 and 1914.

There are a number of axioms that seem to always accurately pertain to warfare. Two of them are: 1) the militaries of the world prepare to fight the next war in the same way the last one ended, and 2) "no plan survives contact with the enemy" (or as Mike Tyson put it more recently, "Everyone's gotta plan until they get punched in the mouth.") Both of these pertained not only to Germany but also to all the combatants to one degree or another.

The Germans were able to mobilize two million men in three weeks. These men were organized into eight armies. Seven of these were sent to implement the Schlieffen Plan and invade France and Belgium, the latter of which had been neutral since 1839 and whose neutrality had been recognized by Prussia and then Germany. The 8th German Army was sent eastward to guard the approaches to Berlin should the Russians mobilize more quickly than anticipated.

The Germans did ask the neutral Belgians for the right to pass through their country on their way to France, a request the Belgians rejected. When they did, Germany invaded the small, relatively flat country and conquered it by the end of August. French and a smaller number of British troops had advanced into Belgium to meet the German push, but by the end of the month, they, along with what was left of the Belgian Army, retreated in near-panic back to France. For a short time, it appeared as if the Germans were going to repeat their victory of 1870/71 and march into Paris,

However, as the bulk of the German Army pushed toward Paris, French resistance stiffened along the Marne River, some twenty miles from the capital. The Battle of the Marne was an indication of the fighting to come: massive and ever-increasing artillery barrages and waves of men cut down by the now mass-produced machine gun. Though the men in the front lines certainly did not know this at the time, the Marne River was as far as the Germans were going to advance into France for the rest of the war.

Illustration 14: Battle of the Marne, 1914. Dotted lines are the furthest German advance. Arrows mark the French counterattack. Courtesy Britannica.com

The Germans were forced to send about sixty thousand soldiers to the Eastern Front because the Russians had been able to mobilize their troops much more rapidly than the Germans had anticipated and were moving toward the German border. The loss of these soldiers when it came to the Battle of the Marne may not have made a difference since the French resistance was incredibly stout. The Russians had moved uncharacteristically fast, and the German commander in the east, General Maximilian von Prittwitz, had made some uncharacteristic mistakes, allowing the Russians to advance farther than anyone imagined they could have.

To remedy this situation, a new commander was appointed to command the German armies in the east: General (later Field Marshal) Paul von Hindenburg. Hindenburg then named an obscure general serving as the commander of the Quartermaster Corps (the section of the army responsible for supplies) as his deputy. His name was Erich Ludendorff. These two would eventually direct the entire German war effort.

The Russians' rapid mobilization was partly due to the planning of Russian generals. Another part was that, contrary to the German Army, many of the Russian soldiers were conscripts with little if any training. And while the Russians did have large numbers of cannons, generally speaking, they were on the move without being fully equipped for battle. As was the case in some situations in the Second World War, many Russian soldiers were sent to the front with very few modern weapons or any weapons at all. Unbelievably, they were told to pick up the weapons of their fallen comrades or those of dead Germans.

Still, at the very beginning of the war, before the fighting started, the Russian Army's morale, for the most part, was high. They were going to fight for the motherland and the tsar, whom many still believed was placed on the throne by God and represented the will of God on Earth. That belief would change more rapidly than anyone could have imagined. The Russian Army moved into the frontier of East Prussia, the hub of German nationalism and the home of most of the General Staff of the German Army.

While the Russian Army did mobilize quickly, it was not able to move as fast as the German Army, and that, combined with the leadership of Hindenburg and Ludendorff, doomed them to defeat in what's known as the Battle of Tannenberg. Although the battle is named this, it actually took place over hundreds of square miles, with the Forest of Tannenberg being only one small part of it.

The area south of Königsberg (today's Kaliningrad) and north of Warsaw is dotted with lakes and forests. Using the terrain to mask their movements, the Germans were able to surround a large part of the Russian force and tear it to pieces. The Russian response to many of the German attacks was to charge, and for the first time in their experience, the Russians faced the massed power of machine guns and rapid-firing cannons.

The Russian losses have been estimated to be between 125,000 and nearly 200,000 dead and wounded, 100,000 prisoners of war, and large numbers of guns and other equipment. The Germans lost just under 15,000 dead, wounded, and missing.

The Battle of Tannenberg not only lifted Hindenburg and Ludendorff to glory but also buoyed the German population, who had expected France to be defeated or nearly defeated at this point in the war (after all, that's what had happened in the war of 1870). Kaiser Wilhelm, who had been facing calls for reform at home before the war and into its first days, decided that from that point on, military victories would justify the continued authoritarian rule of his family. He refused to allow any meaningful reform to happen for the duration of the war, a decision that would come back to haunt him in 1918.

With a couple of disastrous exceptions, the Russians stayed on the defensive for the rest of the war. The offensives that did occur, in 1915 and 1917, only allowed the Germans to drive farther into

Russia and hastened the revolution that had been brewing in Russia since the turn of the century.

Illustration 15: Kaiser Wilhelm II (r) and Tsar Nicholas II of Russia (l), first cousins, wearing each other's uniforms in the years before the war.

Illustration 16: Location of Tannenberg marked with an "X."
Courtesy Britannica.

As you can see from the map on the prior page, the Germans, as well as the Austro-Hungarians, drove deep into Russia, especially Ukraine. Ukraine was a prize the Germans and Austrians sought. Russia's richest agricultural area, complete with large coal deposits, could help the German and Austrian war effort immensely.

By October of 1917, the Russians had suffered nearly nine million dead, wounded, missing, and captured. Over a million of those were civilians. The Germans and Austro-Hungarians had suffered nearly five million dead and wounded.

In that same month, the strength of the Central Powers (Germany, Austria-Hungary, and Turkey, which fought some smaller-scale battles in the Caucasus) stood at nearly 1.3 million, most of those German. If Russia could be removed from the war, those one million or so men could be moved to the Western Front, where the front lines had essentially remained static since the fall of 1914.

Germany was quite aware of the state of the Russian Army from its spies in Russia, the Russian soldiers held in captivity, and the Russian political figures living in exile in Europe. The most prominent of those exiles is a name that is likely familiar to you: Vladimir Ilyich Ulyanov, better known as Lenin, the leader of the radical Bolshevik wing of the Russian Socialist Party.

As reports of various incidents (food riots in Russian cities and towns; soldiers deserting by the hundreds of thousands, sometimes killing the officers who ordered them to attack in another fruitless effort; increasing calls for the tsar to make peace with Germany, which he refused; etc.) reached Germany, the Germans came up with a brilliant plan: they would send Lenin back to Russia to start his revolution. Lenin had openly stated that he felt the war was a conflict between capitalists and aristocrats and that should he come to power, he would immediately take Russia out of the war.

In March 1917, Tsar Nicholas II was forced to abdicate. Alexander Kerensky, the leader of the moderate faction of the Socialist Revolutionary Party, became "Minister-President" of a provisional government. The removal of the tsar was popular, but Kerensky's decision to keep Russia in the war was not.

In April, the Germans allowed Lenin to cross the border from his Swiss exile into Germany. He would go to Sweden, then Finland, and cross the border into Russia to St. Petersburg, the capital of the country. To guard against the chance of Lenin being seen and of his presence stirring up German socialists, the Bolshevik leader was sent to Sweden in a sealed train. In his history of the World War One years, Winston Churchill, who played a major role in both world wars, wrote that the Germans "had turned upon Russia the most grisly of all weapons. They transported Lenin in a sealed truck like a plague bacillus from Switzerland to Russia."

Within a few months, Lenin had rallied his many followers and much of the population of St. Petersburg and staged the Bolshevik Revolution. Among his first accomplishments was taking Russia out of the war.

This was important for Germany for two main reasons. First, they could now shift nearly a million troops from the Eastern Front to the Western Front, where things were bleak, and second, they could impose peace terms on the new Russian government.

The Treaty of Brest-Litovsk, which ended the war on the Eastern Front, was harsh. Its terms called for Russia to give up one million square miles of its territory (mainly in Ukraine but also including parts of western Russia), which held nearly fifty million people. Nearly one-third of Russia's agricultural land was given up, as was a staggering 90 percent of its coal mines. Nearly all her existing oil fields were given to Germany and Austria-Hungary as well.

For his part, Lenin believed it was only a matter of time before either his forces were strong enough to force the Germans from Russia or, more likely, the Germans lost the war in the west and were forced to evacuate anyway. Lenin would prove to be correct with the latter option.

The Western Front and the Home Front in Germany

By the time of Lenin's revolution and the Russian withdrawal from the war, things were beginning to turn against Germany elsewhere. Though the front lines had not shifted much in either direction since the fall of 1914, the cost of the war, both in human and economic terms, was taking a toll on Germany.

The Germans had hoped for a rapid victory in 1914, knowing that any serious prolongation of the conflict played into Allied hands. The Allied Powers, which mainly included France, Great Britain, Russia until 1917, Italy from the spring of 1915, and soon the United States, was too much for Germany to bear alone.

In southeastern Europe, as well as in Russia, the Austro-Hungarian forces were stretched to the limit. The fighting in Russia and Serbia, as well as a grinding campaign of attrition against Italy in the Alps, meant that by 1917, Austria-Hungary was at its breaking point. The many ethnic groups of the Austro-Hungarian Empire were beginning to sense that the empire was teetering on the brink, and many began to form paramilitaries for the time when the empire was no longer strong enough to hold itself together.

The Ottoman Empire, ruled from Constantinople (now Istanbul), was also having a difficult time. The Ottomans, who had already been in decline for more than a century and a half, had fought and won (at great cost) against the British forces at Gallipoli. On top of that, they were not only fighting a losing war in the Middle East and Arabia, where the British were supplying and aiding local forces against the Turks, but were also waging a genocidal campaign against the Armenians in the Caucasus. Both the Austro-Hungarians and Turks were nearly if not completely bankrupt, and the populations of both empires were growing tired of war.

In other words, this meant that Germany was fighting two of the world's greatest powers on its own, and these two powers (Britain and France) would soon be joined by another, the United States.

In Germany itself, the situation was growing worse every day. Despite a controlled press, which essentially told the German public that victory was "just around the corner" for years, people could see and hear for themselves that the situation on the Western Front was not good. They could also feel it in their bodies, for by 1917, the British naval blockade of Germany was beginning to show real results.

The Royal Navy had established the blockade of Germany early in the war. Year by year, the number of ships in the blockade grew. In 1916, Kaiser Wilhelm urged the admirals of the *Kriegsmarine* to challenge the British Grand Fleet (the largest of Britain's many naval formations) in the North Sea and break the blockade. The result was the Battle of Jutland, which ended in a Pyrrhic victory for Germany. The Germans may have sunk more ships and killed more sailors than the British, but the *Kriegsmarine* lost a higher percentage of its total force than the British, who could sustain the losses suffered at Jutland. For the rest of the war, what was left of the German surface fleet stayed in its North Sea ports, where its sailors could see the smoke from the stacks of the British fleet on the horizon, waiting for them to come out.

The British blockade wasn't limited to the area around Germany's access to the sea in the north. All over the world, British ships intercepted, captured, and sometimes sank German merchant ships and others suspected of carrying goods to Germany or German possessions.

The Germans attempted to supply their colonies in the Pacific and Africa by using "surface raiders," armed merchant vessels often flying the colors of a neutral or Allied nation, but after a protracted campaign, virtually all of the "raiders" were captured or sunk. Germany's possessions in the Pacific were lost rather quickly to the Japanese, who had come into the war on the Allied side with the express purpose of seizing German bases in Pacific waters. The British were more than happy with this situation, as it meant they could deploy their fleet elsewhere. (The Americans, who had been anticipating a clash with Japan since the late 1890s, were not so happy.)

By 1917, the blockade and the supply requirements of the army meant that people in Germany were beginning to go hungry, and if there is one thing that rulers know (especially unpopular ones, as the Kaiser was beginning to be), it's that hunger will bring down a government faster than almost anything else.

In response to the British blockade, the Germans set up their own around Great Britain. This was carried out by the new German U-boat (for *Unterseeboot* or "Underseaboat" in English) force. Of course, U-boats were submarines.

The submarine has a much longer history than you may imagine, going all the way back to the mind of Leonardo da Vinci in the 15th and 16th centuries. It saw its first wartime application in the American Civil War, and ever since that time, the prosperous nations of the world had been experimenting with some type of underwater craft. Though most of the great powers of WWI possessed submarines, it was the Germans who made the greatest and most deadly use of them.

Wilhelm's attempt to produce more surface ships was a pipe dream and probably would not have succeeded even in peacetime, but at that time, submarines were relatively easy to build, and what's more, in the First World War, they were virtually undetectable while submerged. To counter the British blockade and hopefully cause some of the ships blockading German ports to redeploy, the Germans mounted a counter-blockade of Great Britain using their U-boat force.

Today, we might chuckle at the naivete of the combatants of WWI in regard to U-boat warfare, but in 1916, submarine warfare was new—the rules "governing" "civilized" behavior at sea were not. The last international conference to meet and revise the rules of naval warfare had taken place in 1856, which was before Germany was even a united nation and before submarines were a practical reality. Those rules required that any vessel attempting to "run" a blockade could not be attacked until it had been stopped or warned by a "shot across the bow" and after an inspection of its cargo and provisions arranged for its crew (whether that was a rescue in lifeboats or being taken aboard the attacking ship).

As you are likely aware by now, there was no way a submarine could abide by those rules and survive. Any ship, merchant or otherwise, armed with a heavy machine gun, not to mention a light naval cannon, could pierce the hull of these early wartime submarines. After some experience in submarine warfare, the British and others found the only reliable defense against submarines to be the "convoy system," in which large numbers of merchantmen would be escorted by naval vessels. Since the U-boats depended on stealth, a formal warning to the crew and an inspection was out, as was taking any survivors aboard. At times, U-boats did radio neutral nations as to the positions of sunken ships (the idea being that these neutral nations would forward them to the British or whomever), but that rarely happened.

Lastly, it must be remembered that the U-boats of WWI had a submerged speed of only about eight knots (nine miles per hour), depending on conditions, and could only stay submerged for about five hours before they had to surface to both charge their batteries and replenish their oxygen supply. For the most part, U-boats, with their very low profile and grayish-black color, would approach convoys or lone merchantmen on the surface, preferably at night, dusk, or dawn, taking full advantage of their construction. Most times, torpedo attacks would be launched from the surface rather than from below the water for greater accuracy. Traveling underwater, while perfect for evasion in survival situations, was really a last resort, which was exactly why the Germans announced they would not abide by the 1856 naval treaty terms, claiming they were outdated and unfair.

Of course, the Allies argued the opposite, exclaiming that submarine warfare was cruel and illegal and making the U-boat crews out to be the worst kind of criminals.

For the first two years of the war, the Germans had attempted to wage "restricted submarine warfare." This meant that they would attempt to avoid attacks on the shipping of neutral nations, especially American shipping. "Accidents" happened, however, most notably the sinking of the British liner *Lusitania* off the coast of Ireland in April 1915, which took nearly 1,200 lives (128 of them American). The Germans argued that they had warned everyone not to board ships bound for the British Isles, which they did. The Americans exclaimed that as neutrals, they had the right to go anywhere. The British accused Germany of sinking a passenger liner that was not carrying war materiel, which was definitely not true, though British propaganda was effective in causing people to believe their message. Not wanting the Americans to enter the war on the side of the Allies (and, in 1915, it was not a foregone conclusion they would), the Germans "apologized" and announced their commitment to restricted submarine warfare.

However, by 1917, with the land war at a standstill and the British blockade taking a toll, the Germans announced unrestricted submarine warfare on all vessels entering British waters. They hoped that by the time the United States entered the war on the side of the Allies, the U-boats would have forced the British, at the very least, to the peace table.

The Germans' U-boat warfare enraged the world, and it was a factor in the United States' entry into the war, though it was not the direct cause, which we will discuss in a moment.

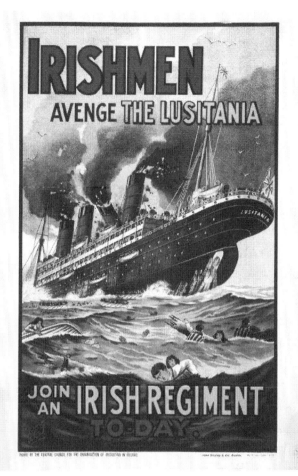

Illustration 17: This British poster (all of Ireland was then a British possession) depicts the sinking of the Lusitania. At the time, the images were considered "shocking."

Illustration 18: "Boats out!" German propaganda illustrating the effectiveness and vitality of the U-boat force.

By the beginning of 1917, the war on the Western Front had been in a stalemate for nearly three years. After the Battle of the Marne, both sides began the famous Race to the Sea, which were attempts to outmaneuver each other by outflanking the other's forces by moving northward toward the English Channel. Soon, however, the combat in France and a very small piece of unoccupied Belgium bogged down into the infamous "trench warfare" for which WWI is known.

Until almost the very end of the war, outdated tactics were used to overcome the newest wartime technology, which included machine guns, rapid-firing artillery, and poison gas. The result was a bloodbath that was only imagined by a few forward-thinking people before the war started. For everyone else, WWI shocked them psychologically, emotionally, and physically.

Toward the end of the war, the invention of the tank threatened to change the way the war was fought, but old thinking and poor reliability made the tank more of a weapon of the future than of 1917 and 1918 when it was deployed on the battlefield for the first time. Even then, military men were not sure of its potential.

They were, however, aware of the potential of the airplane, which had been invented just years before the outbreak of the war. Aerial warfare first involved the use of planes (along with hot-air and hydrogen balloons and dirigibles) for reconnaissance, but soon, it evolved into reconnaissance pilots shooting at each other with pistols and dropping grenades or small bombs on the cannons or rifles shooting at them from the ground. The airplane evolved quickly. Machine guns were attached to the rear of two-seater planes; later, forward-firing machine guns were made possible by the invention of the interrupter gear, which made it possible to shoot through propeller blades. Then heavier and heavier bombers were developed to attack munitions depots, troop transports, and, eventually, population centers (though most of this was done very late in the war and mostly by dirigibles or the German Zeppelins).

The most well-known of all the warriors of WWI were the fighter pilots, who seemed to embody the spirit of another age. All sides called them the "Knights of the Air," and the single combat they engaged each other in was reminiscent of a simpler and less brutal time. The most famous of them all was the German ace Manfred von Richthofen, also known as the "Red Baron," who had eighty-one kills. After the Red Baron's death in April 1918, a skilled but arrogant flyer named Hermann Göring, who would rise to command the German Air Force in WWII, took over the Baron's command of the famous "Flying Circus" squadron.

Illustration 19: Colorized portrait of von Richthofen wearing his "Blue Max," the Pour le Mérite, *instituted by the French-speaking king of Prussia, Frederick the Great.*

On April 6th, 1917, US President Woodrow Wilson signed the declaration of war against Germany (and later Austria-Hungary, although not one against the Ottoman Empire, the third of the Central Powers). Wilson had resisted many calls to engage in the war before that time. Though the sinking of the *Lusitania* and other incidents on the high seas were the most emotionally charged reasons for the Americans declaring war, the immediate reason was another German miscalculation and error: the Zimmermann Telegram.

Simply put, in January 1917, German Foreign Secretary Arthur Zimmermann cabled his ambassador in Mexico and told him to propose to the Mexican government that Mexico declare war on the United States. In return, Germany would support Mexico's war effort and ensure that the Mexicans received their former territories of Texas, New Mexico, and Arizona, which they had lost to the United States in the Mexican-American War.

At the time, this was taken as a very serious threat, as the United States and Mexico had essentially been at war with each other immediately before and during the first part of WWI. US forces had been in Mexico chasing Mexican guerrillas and bandits who had been raiding across the border for some time, both for riches and to finance their struggle against the Mexican government, which was no longer friendly with the US. When WWI broke out, the standing Mexican Army was larger than that of the United States.

Not only had Germany sunk American ships and killed American citizens on the high seas and interfered with American commerce, now they were threatening America's borders directly. The Zimmermann Telegram, which was intercepted by British intelligence and decoded, was the last straw. The US declared war, and Germany's fate was sealed. (Foreign Minister Zimmermann himself confirmed the contents of the telegram publicly, which was yet another German error.)

It would take months for the US to get itself on a war footing. In actuality, it took about a year before enough American troops were in Europe to make their presence felt. With the Russians dropping out of the war in late 1917 and the time it would take for the Americans to build, train, equip, and transport an adequate force to Europe, Germany realized it had a very short window to achieve a victorious change in the war.

German Politics

Before we delve into the last German offensive of the war, let's take a moment to discuss what was happening within Germany and its political life in the latter part of the war.

By 1917, especially after the American entry into the war, many of Germany's elite knew the war was lost. The stalemate on the Western Front showed no signs of changing, and the British and French, while sustaining great casualties like the Germans, were able to build more and more munitions as time went by. In contrast,

German funds were running out, while the British and French were being subsidized and supplied by the United States. The numerical superiority of the Allies (especially when one considers Italy and both Britain and France's colonial troops, of which there were over a million) combined with the dwindling manpower of Germans painted a bleak picture for Germany. Even after Germany failed to take Paris in 1914, the Kaiser's own son and heir, Crown Prince Wilhelm, had admitted that Germany could not win the war.

Within Germany, people were getting mixed messages. Troops coming home on leave and those in the hospital told tales of horror, supply shortages, and ever-increasing numbers of Allied troops. During the course of the war on the Western Front, a German unit might find itself fighting English, Irish, Scottish, Welsh, French, Canadians, Australians, New Zealanders, Algerians, Congolese, Belgians, Moroccans, and others. This happened to many units, and the Germans began to feel they were fighting against the whole world and growing more weary of it every day.

Both sides felt the uselessness of the attack or "going over the top," which was what cresting the top of the trench was referred to back then. In the Battle of the Somme, British troops lost 30,000 men in *one day*. During the Battle of Verdun, which German generals had hoped would suck in more and more French troops and eventually break the morale of France, cost the Germans nearly 400,000 killed and wounded, with a relatively equal number of Frenchmen. And, in the end, French morale held. By 1917/1918, many within Germany were wishing for an end.

However, the problem was this, and it was felt to some degree by both liberals and conservatives alike: the war couldn't simply end. Too many had sacrificed for that to happen so easily. Germany had to get something for its efforts, whether it be land, reparations, or colonies.

The problem was that no one within Germany could picture the Allies making peace in which Germany gained something. After all, those countries had also sacrificed too. The only alternative, it seemed (and it was met with either resignation or zeal, depending on where you were on the political spectrum), was one last push for all-out victory, which had to take place before the arrival of significant numbers of fresh American troops and their tons of equipment.

1918 Offensive

In the spring of 1918, Germany launched a powerful offensive dubbed the Ludendorff Offensive for the man who had planned it. Both Ludendorff and Hindenburg, who was now in command of Germany's entire effort in the west, believed the casualties for the offensive would reach over half a million men, but they thought that the strength of the drive and its theoretical gains would force the Allies to the negotiating table and give Germany favorable peace terms.

The spearhead of the offensive was a unit dubbed *Sturmtruppen* or "Stormtroopers," and they had been trained in new ways of attacking and exploiting the opponents' trenches. In truth, not only the Germans but also their allies, the Austro-Hungarians, as well as the Allied Powers, had all trained these types of units, but it was the Germans who used them in the greatest quantity and most effectively in the first days of the Spring Offensive of 1918.

As opposed to most of the other major offensives of the war, Ludendorff ordered a short, intense artillery barrage, behind which the Stormtroopers would follow closely. This was not a new tactic, but it proved most effective. Allied troops, who were in a daze from the short barrage (as opposed to the long hours or days-long barrages that would previously have signaled an attack), would emerge from their dugouts to find specially trained, equipped, and highly motivated German troops inside their lines.

Carrying shotguns, small machine guns, dozens of grenades, and carrying hand-to-hand weapons that looked like they came from the Dark Ages, the Stormtroopers would create a breakthrough in the Allied trenches, allowing the rest of their comrades to rush through, then file in behind the Allied lines to the left and right. This went on through the many lines of trenches until the Germans almost reached open country. In many ways, it was the infantry precursor of the blitzkrieg tank attacks that would take place in WWII (in fact, many commanders of the blitzkrieg attacks were WWI combat veterans).

Unfortunately for the Germans, several things happened. One of their aims was to capture Allied supplies, for, after a number of weeks, the Germans' supplies had run out. Another problem that is not spoken of frequently but which you will find in the specialized literature on the subject (two of which are listed in the bibliography) is that many of the first line Stormtroopers were captured after having broken through and raiding French field kitchens and food supplies. In many cases, the French returned to find dozens of drunk and sick German soldiers, who, after being deprived by shortages on their side of the lines, stuffed and drank themselves into a stupor.

Still, the drive was serious, and for a time, it worried the Allied command, but three things happened to the Allies' advantage. French and British resistance stiffened, the Germans exhausted both themselves and their supplies, and the Americans began arriving on the battlefield in consequential numbers.

For the Germans, the arrival of considerable numbers of Americans meant the end was near. Both Hindenburg and Ludendorff, as well as most of their fellow generals, knew the war was over. At first, the Americans made blunder after blunder on the battlefield, fighting as green troops, but they learned quickly, both from their own experience and from the British and French, who were on both sides of the American front lines. More importantly were the over two million Americans waiting on piers and in training grounds in the United States waiting to go "Over There," as the popular American fight song went. Even more significant than the millions of American troops were the seemingly endless supply of ammunition and other supplies that the Americans brought with them and financed for the British and French.

In the early fall of 1918, the British and French, their spirits somewhat renewed by both the holding of the German offensive and the arrival of the Americans, began new offensives all along the Western Front. By late September, Hindenburg and Ludendorff knew it was only a matter of time before complete German collapse. On September 29th, they approached Kaiser Wilhelm II at his retreat near Spa in western Germany and urged him to approach the Allies for an armistice while German troops were still in possession of French and Belgian territories.

That armistice took place on November 11th, 1918.

Chapter 5 – The Treaty of Versailles

There is perhaps no more infamous peace treaty than that of the Treaty of Versailles, which officially ended World War One. While in 1918, the Allied Powers and their citizens cheered the armistice and the treaty that ended the war, within just a few years, many in Britain, France, and the US were beginning to wonder if the Treaty of Versailles had been too hard on the Germans. By the early to mid-1920s, a variety of political groups had risen in Germany, whose main platform was the rejection of the Versailles Treaty and its "onerous" terms. Obviously, the most well-known of these was the National Socialist German Workers' Party (also known as the *Nationalsozialistische Deutsche Arbeiterpartei*, the NSDAP, or the Nazi Party, named from the German pronunciation of the first two words), but many parties and organizations, both large and small, nationwide and local, were vocal opponents of the treaty. During the 1920s, it seemed as if the hatred of the Treaty of Versailles was the one thing that most Germans could agree on.

So, was the Treaty of Versailles "unfair" to Germany? The answer is both yes and no, but before the treaty (which was really several separate agreements bundled together) was even inked, there had to be an armistice. The ceasefire that effectively ended WWI was where the problems began.

In the last months of the war, the Social Democratic Party (SPD), the largest in Germany, had been gaining both strength and influence. Though their platform was multi-faceted, by September 1918, it consisted of one thing: ending the war.

Throughout most of the war, the SPD was divided against itself. A large percentage of its members were completely against the war, seeing it as another war of the ruling classes of one nation or kingdom against another with the "little man" used as cannon fodder. There was a conservative wing of the party that did support the war wholeheartedly, but they were a distinct minority. Most of its members supported the war effort as "good Germans," but as the conflict wore on and victory seemed to elude the German Army, more and more members of the SPD wanted to find a way out.

When peace was discussed in September 1918, it was decided that any peace overture had to come from the leading politicians of the SPD. Members of the military were reluctant for a number of reasons, including the notion that the Allies would be less willing to accept a peace overture coming from the military. Another issue would also rear its ugly head, for while it was the military that urged approaching the Allies, it was the SPD and the politicians who actually made the overture. In the coming months and years, many who had been or were in the German Army (including, hypocritically, Erich Ludendorff) accused the politicians of "selling out" the German soldier. To these men, the politicians had basically stabbed them in the back when victory was around the corner.

But a victory was not around the corner, even though the highly censored German newspapers kept saying so, as did the generals to their troops. They kept mentioning the fact that German soldiers continued to occupy foreign soil while Germany itself stood inviolate. They promoted the idea that the Germans were winning the war, but as you can see from the previous chapter, this was not the case.

The truth was that supplies were running low, the Americans were fully in the war, the Allies were about to crack the German front lines, and, in October 1918, leftist revolutions broke out in Germany, most significantly among sailors at the naval base at Kiel. Germany could not, and most Germans would not, go on. That was the reality.

On the eleventh hour of the eleventh day of the eleventh month, the ceasefire took place, and for all intents and purposes, World War One was over. The Kaiser abdicated on November 9th and went into exile in Holland, where he lived in relative luxury while his country suffered the consequences of a lost war, which was, in part, brought about by his decision to support Austria. He died in 1940, relatively forgotten, during the first years of WWII.

Within a few months, German soldiers, sometimes with orders, sometimes without, began to filter home. Some of them were sent to areas within Germany to help put down the communist uprisings taking place in some of the cities. Many just went home to a country in economic and political shambles.

The Paris Peace Conference and the Treaty of Versailles

One of the largest issues facing the Allies when the Paris Peace Conference began was who was to blame for starting the war. In reality, the Serbian Black Hand movement started it, but since the king of Serbia had repudiated the actions of the Black Hand and since Serbia was an Allied nation, that left the rest of the Central Powers to shoulder the blame for the carnage of World War One.

Unfortunately, for the Germans, they were the "last man standing," as it were. The Austro-Hungarian Empire had come apart at the seams in the last months of the war, and as the Paris Peace Conference met to not only make peace but also to establish borders in the new post-war Europe, the many ethnic groups of the former Habsburg Empire were either sitting down at the negotiating table themselves or were on the battlefield attempting to form their own nations out of what had been one of the largest empires in Europe.

Almost the same situation existed in the now-former Ottoman Empire. Throughout the war, the British (and, to some degree, the French) had worked to rally the people of the Middle East against their Ottoman masters centered in Turkey. The most famous example of this is the exploits of Lawrence of Arabia in today's Saudi Arabia, but there were similar examples in other Ottoman lands. When the war ended, there was no longer an Ottoman Empire, and it took years for the major powers, which had begun to realize the potential of Middle Eastern oil fields, to draw the lines on the map that we know today, with one exception: Israel. The Turks formed a new country, but it took a nearly genocidal war with the Greeks, which lasted from 1920 to 1922, in order to establish their borders permanently.

That left Germany. Germany had not been invaded. Its borders were intact, as were its factories, coal fields, and farms, which were some of the richest in the world. Add to that the important point that the Kaiser had issued the infamous "blank check" to Austria-Hungary in support of their war against Serbia. Without that, there likely would not have been a war, at least not a global one. Finally, the Germans had inflicted the most damage of any of the Central Powers. Millions were dead, and industries had been picked apart or destroyed in the areas that had been under German control. What's more, Germany had invaded France twice in fifty years. Germany would pay, at least as far as the Allies were concerned.

Politicians and citizens in Germany expected something different. They were willing to accept the idea that their nation might have to pay some reparations, and most were willing to give up Alsace-Lorraine or at least part of it. They were completely deluded. What's more, some of the more conservative members of

German society believed that Germany should be allowed to retain the lands it had won from Russia in the Treaty of Brest-Litovsk (a treaty, it should be remembered, that was severe in comparison to what eventually became the Treaty of Versailles).

The way the German delegation was treated during the peace conference should have given some clue as to what the nature of the final peace treaty would be like. When German diplomats attempted to insert themselves into conversations and negotiations, they were shut out almost completely unless it was to answer a question or provide data.

What about the Allies? Simply put, the French wanted revenge and were prepared to resume the war if they didn't get what they wanted, which was an amazingly large amount of money, Alsace-Lorraine, and control over the coal-producing regions of western Germany for a specified period as a guarantee of at least some payment.

The Americans also believed that the Germans should pay reparations for the war, although it was a far lesser number than the French. They believed that Alsace-Lorraine should be French and that the German Army should be limited in size for at least the near future, with which both the French and British agreed.

The British fell somewhere in between the American and French positions, and in the end, they leaned more toward France than America, a position that many in the United Kingdom would come to see as a mistake in the coming years.

It should be noted that when the German politicians approached the Allies, they approached the Americans, believing that they would receive more lenient terms from a nation that had just entered the war and had not suffered the great casualties that the British and French had. They were also mindful of the rhetoric coming from US President Woodrow Wilson, whose speeches contained frequent references to making WWI "the war to end all wars" and constructing a plan for world peace—forever.

When Wilson arrived in France, he was a superstar. Literally millions of people came out to see him. His country had come to the Allies' aid in their time of need, financed the war, and now apparently had a plan to make wars a thing of the past. This last item proved to be the sticking point for Wilson, for to get what eventually became his Fourteen Points passed and to end the conflict in Europe and war forever, he was willing to give France and Britain almost exactly what they wanted.

For about six months, the eyes of the world were on Paris. In May, a finished draft was handed to the Germans for their comments. To say that the Germans, both within and outside the government, were shocked would be putting it mildly. This was made worse by the fact that the Germans' lengthy reply, which was delivered in June, was rejected almost completely. Essentially, the Germans were faced with two choices: sign or the war begins anew.

Though some on the German right exclaimed they were willing to fight to the death rather than see their government sign the treaty, that was both hot air and an impossibility. By the summer of 1919, the German Army no longer existed, at least not in any form that could resist an Allied invasion in any way. Aside from that, there was still revolution in the streets of major cities, hunger, unemployment, and inflation. Germany was spent, and the Allies knew it.

During this period, the dangerous stab-in-the-back myth (*Dolchstoß* in German) began. Like most lies, it began with a kernel of truth. On November 11th, 1918, when, for all intents and purposes, the war ended, no Allied force stood on German soil. Quite the contrary—German troops were still in possession of large parts of northern France and most of Belgium, although they were rapidly being driven back when the ceasefire took place. The

German Army didn't lose the war; rather, it was the politicians who lost it.

As you will recall, it was Generals Hindenburg and Ludendorff, among and others, who approached Kaiser Wilhelm II and recommended that he pursue peace. Now, it seemed, they knew nothing about that. According to them, it had been pressure from the Social Democrats who forced the end of the war (in time, the Jewish heads of some of Germany's banks were seen as the culprits as well). On top of that, the mismanagement of the war economy by the politicians caused a lack of supply. However, it was the German Army and the Kaiser's office that were essentially in command of the war economy from the start, meaning they were the ones that had managed it poorly.

Still, except for the most deluded, most Germans knew they had no choice. They had to sign the treaty. What's worse, the sum of reparations had not even been finalized when the treaty was presented. An unreal figure of 632 billion marks had been announced previously (this would equate to about two trillion in US dollars today), but eventually, that huge sum was whittled down to a still staggering (especially for the time and for an economy in shambles) 132 billion marks (approximately 400 billion US dollars today).

Among the major points of the Treaty of Versailles as they pertained to Germany were the aforementioned reparations, the return of Alsace-Lorraine to France, the demilitarization of the left bank of the Rhine River (meaning no German troops in the area bordering France), giving France the total production of the Saar Basin coal deposits for twenty years, and the stipulation that if Germany defaulted on its payments, both France and Belgium (which had been occupied by Germany for four years and its economy stripped of virtually all industry) had the right to occupy the industrial heart of Germany, the Ruhr Valley in western Germany. Germany's borders in the east were also to be moved about one hundred miles westward, and East Prussia would be separated from the rest of the country by the reemergence of Poland, which had been under German/Prussian, Austrian, and Russian control since the 18th century. Millions of Germans were forced to move from their homes, rich and poor alike. To say this was resented is an understatement.

Germany also forfeited all its overseas colonies, and, possibly the worst of all, the German Army was limited in size to 100,000 men. There was to be no air force, and Germany was allowed only a limited coastal defense navy.

Though the reparations were probably the worst part of the terms of the treaty (by the way, Germany paid the last of its reparations payments in 2010), psychologically, the limits to the armed forces were likely the worst.

As you may remember, the army had been a pillar of German life since the days of the kings of Prussia, and it wasn't just in Prussia that the military was held in high regard or even awe—this held true in many of the German states before 1870. With the unification of Germany in 1871, largely due to the outcome of victorious wars, the army held an almost revered status in Germany. Of course, by the end of the First World War, this feeling had begun to change, especially in the larger cities, where progressive political parties and populations saw the army as a tool of the Kaiser. Arch-conservatives used the army to keep the progressives down. However, for the majority of the people in the country, the army was respected and admired.

The strength of the pre-war German Army was about 750,000 men. This is sort of a deceiving figure since, due to the structure of the draft and length of service required, almost all able-bodied German men served in the army at some point. And when their time in active duty was done, they were put in reserve and were subject to relatively regular training and exercises. Many times, those who became officers made the army a lifelong career. Even in retirement, a captain would not be addressed as *Herr Schmidt* ("Mr. Schmidt"), for example, but as *Herr Kapitän Schmidt* to the day he died. With the stroke of a pen, the Allies ended the future of many German men. To compensate for this loss, among other reasons, many German men joined paramilitary groups. Obviously, the most well known are those of the extreme right wing, such as Hitler's *Sturmabteilung* ("Storm Section" or "Storm Detachment"), better known by its acronym, SA, and its predecessor, the *Freikorps* or "Free Corps." However, a variety of other political groups had their own paramilitaries as well, especially the KPD (*Kommunistiche Partei Deutschlands*, the Communist Party of Germany), with their *Rotfront* ("Red Front") groups.

The German Navy was ordered to sail for Scapa Flow, Britain's largest naval base, in the north of Scotland. Once there, the ships' crews scuttled (destroyed) their ships rather than have them sail under a British flag. The German Navy, which had once been the pride of Kaiser Wilhelm, only existed in a number of coastal patrol vessels. It was not allowed to have any submarines.

The German Air Force was eliminated completely, and no one was able to obtain a pilot's license. The Allies wanted to give the Germans only enough troops to keep order within their own borders and nothing more. Strangely enough, and in relatively rapid fashion, the German General Staff, led by General Hans von Seeckt, organized secret training fields in, of all places, the Soviet Union. Germans who wanted to become pilots soon learned a "workaround"; they learned to fly gliders, which were not restricted by the Versailles Treaty. Many of the *Luftwaffe* aces of WWII learned to fly gliders in the 1920s.

And on top of all of this was the infamous (for the Germans, at any rate) Article 231 of the peace treaty. This clause laid the blame for World War One entirely on Germany. To the Allies, this, of course, justified all of the restrictions listed above and more, but Article 231 had a psychological effect on the German nation as well.

The article was named the War Guilt Clause, but the idea that the Allies, who mobilized their armies at the same time as Germany and who came to the aid of Serbian assassins, would blame the Germans for the entire war caused resentment in Germany, which would simmer and boil until well after Hitler was elected chancellor in 1933.

Illustration 20: "Germany's children are hungry!" Sketch/poster by famed German artist Kathe Kollwitz, 1923 (courtesy https://www.kollwitz.de/en/germany-s-children-are-starving-kn-202).

Chapter 6 – The Weimar Republic

Between February and June 1919, a new national assembly of Germany met in the central-eastern German city of Weimar to put together a new constitution. The Kaiser had fled to Holland, and the army, while still an organized entity, was in shambles after the war. Some on the right wanted the new government to be run by the generals, but neither the vast majority of Germans nor (more importantly) the Allies would have tolerated that.

The Weimar Assembly was dominated by the SPD (the Social Democratic Party), though other parties, both large and small, were represented. The most significant of these was the Centre Party, which represented the Catholics of Germany. The Communist Party was not involved or wanted; at the time, various, somewhat autonomous branches of the Communist Party were busy trying to establish a "dictatorship of the Proletariat" (the working class) in cities around Germany. This happened in Hamburg, parts of Bavaria (which was becoming a right-wing haven), and cities and towns in Saxony in the east and the Rhineland and Ruhr area in the western part of the country.

The most serious of these uprisings happened in Berlin. It began on January 5th, 1919, and was led by the most militant wing of the German Communist Party, the Spartacist League, named after the famed Roman slave who led a rebellion from 71 to 73 BCE. Its leaders were Rosa Luxemburg and Karl Liebknecht. Both had been members of the Social Democratic Party and its more leftist offshoot, the Independent Social Democratic Party (known in German as the *Unabhängige Sozialdemokratische Partei Deutschlands* or the USPD). However, they both broke from them when the SPD voted to support the war. Both became quite radical as the war went on, to the point of criticizing Leninism in Russia and the socialists around Europe. Luxemburg, Liebknecht, and the SPD had taken part in the sporadic fighting that broke out at the end of the war, which helped result in the end of the war, the abdication of the Kaiser, and the armistice.

During that time, they turned their considerable talents to organizing the Spartacist League and its newspaper, *Die Rote Fahne* or "The Red Flag," and attempted to put together a paramilitary group that could resist the numerous right-wing paramilitaries beginning to sprout up all over Germany.

The Spartacist uprising in Berlin developed rather spontaneously out of a march against the police, which grew from a few thousand to hundreds of thousands of people. Some people in the crowd were armed with firearms, knives, or tools. During the march on January 5th, differing groups occupied offices of the ruling SPD, as well as various newspapers run by the SPD and more conservative parties, which had been calling for the violent suppression of the communists in Berlin.

Amid the chaos, fifty-three leading members of the Communist Party and the Spartacist League met to form a provisional government of Berlin, but they were divided in both purpose and goals. Karl Liebknecht called for the armed overthrow of the country's government. Rosa Luxemburg considered the entire enterprise an unorganized fiasco and made a speech against it, but she did join in the call for a general strike on January 7th.

When this strike of nearly 500,000 people or more began, elements began to both attack government buildings (and take over many) and call on the army and police to join them. Talks went on between Prime Minister Friedrich Ebert, his defense minister, and the representatives of the strikers throughout most of the day, but they ended in a stalemate. At that point, the Spartacists announced they would take up arms against the government.

The entire episode would likely have played itself out much more peacefully had cooler heads prevailed. After all, the Spartacists had no real support outside Berlin, at least none that could get to them, and even within Berlin, people were tired of the violence and suffering. Had the government made a few concessions about working conditions, the armed uprising likely would not have taken place.

However, with the call for violence and similar events occurring in other cities, along with concerns that the army might move in and take power should the SPD government not move against the communists, Ebert called in both the military and various branches of right-wing paramilitaries calling themselves the *Freikorps*. The *Freikorps* was composed mostly of combat veterans, with almost all of them still armed with weapons from the war. These groups had sprouted up all over Germany and were secretly funded by the government, at times with the urging of the Western Allies, who were not keen on seeing a communist takeover of Germany.

The suppression of the Spartacists in Berlin took about a week, at times with pitched battles (including field mortars) going on in the streets. Both Luxemburg and Liebknecht were found in an apartment building and arrested. Liebknecht was beaten bloody and shot three times, his body later being sent to the morgue naked and unidentified until later. Shortly thereafter, Rosa Luxemburg was brought through the lobby of a building, where she was hit twice in the head with a rifle butt and then beaten further by a gang of *Freikorps* men. She was taken to the back of a truck and shot in the back of the head, her body dumped in the nearby Landwehr Canal. It was not found until later that summer.

The Spartacist uprising was a disaster from the start, but it has taken a larger place in history than what it actually effected. Like the hyperinflation that was to follow, the uprising terrified both the government and many citizens of Germany, most of whom, especially outside the poorer areas of the bigger cities, were conservative or moderate in outlook. They remembered a time before the war when Germany was the most prosperous country in Europe, and they believed the communists threatened a rebuilding of that economy, especially under the terms of the Treaty of Versailles.

They also saw the uprising and communism in general as being inspired by Russia and "foreign forces," which literally meant foreigners but also very pointedly meant Jews. Karl Marx, though an atheist, was born a German Jew, and many of the Russian revolutionaries who took over Russia in 1917 were Jewish, which is no surprise. In a nation that had known virulent anti-Semitic pogroms for centuries, communism, with its call for universal brotherhood, would have been highly appealing. Lastly, Rosa Luxemburg, though a naturalized German citizen, was a Polish Jew by origin. In right-wing newspapers and flyers before the uprising, she was often referred to not simply as Rosa Luxemburg but as "The Jew, Rosa Luxemburg" or "The Polish Jew." In years to come, even before the rise of the Nazis, the impact of the violence not only in Berlin but also throughout Germany caused an uptick in anti-Semitic language and violence.

Throughout Germany, the *Freikorps* violently and sometimes atrociously put down communist uprisings, killed leaders, and intimidated the population. In the border areas between Germany and Poland, a vicious low-level war took place, with atrocities being committed on both sides, which, of course, fueled greater hatreds yet to come.

Illustration 21: Freikorps' recruiting poster: *"Comrade! Help me against Bolshevism, the Polish danger and starvation."* Dated from the time of the Spartacist uprising.

The *Freikorps* were eventually suppressed by the army at the order of the government and with the urging of the Allies. They had become too numerous and were showing a willingness to defy the government when it suited them. The level of violence committed by many of the *Freikorps* units also frightened many in Germany. As the years went by, a great number of the *Freikorps* went on to join the Nazi SA, where their violent tendencies were encouraged. Similarly, the communists also formed their own paramilitary, consisting of workers and a considerable number of war veterans. These two forces would wage war in the streets of German cities with increasing regularity and violence in the later years of the 1920s and early 1930s.

Not long after the uprisings, Germany was faced with another threat, this one more serious: France.

In November of 1922, Germany was unable to pay the second installment of the reparations required by the Treaty of Versailles. Talks produced no solutions, and as stipulated in the treaty, on December 27th, 1922, the French and Belgians moved troops into the industrial Ruhr area of Germany. Troops took over the region's coal mines, factories, and railways. Naturally, there were incidents between French and Belgian troops and Germans, a couple of which you can view on YouTube.

In response to the Franco-Belgian occupation, the German government told workers to use tactics of "passive resistance" against the occupiers. They refused to show up to work, and if they did show up, they immediately went home or sabotaged the machinery. At the massive Krupp steelworks, tensions between workers and French troops escalated to the point of bloodshed, with French soldiers firing on German protesters. At this point, the German government, now run by Prime Minister Gustav Stresemann, promised to pay the wages of the workers in the area.

Hindsight is 20/20, as they say, and had the French and Belgians been a bit more flexible in their demands, the entire situation might have been avoided. However, in June 1922, the very able and popular German foreign minister, Walther Rathenau, a Jewish German, had been assassinated by right-wing extremists linked to the *Freikorps* (another reason for their disbandment) for having engaged in talks with the Soviet Union (which were actually beneficial to Germany). Rathenau was an able minister, and he was respected not only in Germany but also by the Allies. His death was a huge blow.

Let's take a moment to consider the impact of the reparations payments on Germany and German businesses. Governments receive money in a variety of ways, but two of the prime ways are through taxation and bonds (think of these as long-term loans). When the reparations repayment period began, the German government was broke and had been for some time. In fact, almost the entire war effort had been conducted on credit. Of course, when the government fell apart and defaulted, many banks went with it, as did people's life savings. Businesses could no longer get loans, and they could neither pay taxes nor people's salaries. This hit businesses both large and small. Some of the world's largest industrial companies either went broke or were nearly broke by the early 1920s.

Unfortunately, to make matters worse, the government had to raise taxes, for instance, placing taxes on foodstuffs that individual consumers bought but could no longer afford. Businesses, to make up for the shortfall they were paying in taxes, had to raise their prices. When prices go up and the value of currency goes down, you have inflation. Eventually, the German government was trying to get blood from a stone, and when they did get paid, that money had lost its value. However, they still passed what they could on to the Allies in their first installment under the Versailles Treaty.

Now, throw into the mix a fateful decision made by the German government to fulfill their promise to pay the workers of the Ruhr and other regions affected by the occupation and passive resistance—they printed more money. Today, we know the effects of this precisely because of this time period. The policy-makers of the German government did, too, to an extent, but the 1920s was a time when many governments were changing from currencies based on gold to a fiat system, which was essentially currency based on demand and the market. As a result, these policy-makers were not completely aware of the nightmare they were creating. This nightmare was the German Hyperinflation of 1922/23.

Many doctors of economics have written their doctoral theses on the German Hyperinflation, and thousands of books have been written about this very brief but nightmarish situation. Suffice it to say here that if you have one of an object, especially if it's the only one, it's very valuable. By printing more money, the German government was reducing the value people put on money every time the printing presses rolled on—and they rolled on, and on, and on. Soon, inflation was so out of control that people were literally being paid to show up to work and again at lunch, for between the hours of 8 and 12, money had lost its value hundreds of times over. At the height of the hyperinflation, the German government was issuing bills in the amount of *one hundred trillion* mark notes.

Say, for example, you had ten thousand marks in the bank. Before the war, this would've been worth roughly two or three thousand US dollars. During hyperinflation, you couldn't buy a loaf of bread for ten thousand marks. People's savings went up in smoke. People got paid millions of marks, which means landlords then suffered since rents stayed the same. If you had a long-term lease that called for twenty marks a month, well, that was easy to pay, but the landlord was then left with a twenty mark note, which was worth less than a modern-day penny. He had to pay his mortgage with money he did not have, and thus, the chain went on and on.

People went hungry and lost their jobs; no one knows exactly how many people starved to death. Soup kitchens were opened all over Germany, usually run by churches or the International Red Cross. People's pride went out the window, and the country's pride went out the window. As a result of all this, people began to flock toward the communists and the parties of the extreme right.

Illustration 22: Hyperinflation bill from July 1923

Eventually, the government issued a new currency, the Rentenmark, which was actually based on the American dollar. This, as well as other steps taken over the course of 1923, finally ended the economic turmoil, but the damage had been done. The hyperinflation left a huge scar on the collective German psyche. When the Great Depression struck in 1929, the nightmare of 1923 came rushing back into the German consciousness, and people began to make choices based on fear.

Illustration 23: German making a withdrawal from a bank in 1923. A popular rumor was that a man had taken a wagon to the bank to get his money. He was held up, and the thieves took the wagon but left the pile of money. Women would go into a store to buy a sack of potatoes carrying bags of money. Thieves would watch them go in with the money and take the potatoes, which were worth far more, for food or trade.

The hyperinflation was a wake-up call, not only for Germany but also for the Western Allies. They knew that if Germany went through too many economic earthquakes, she might turn to communism, for with every jolt to the economy, more people joined the far-left (and the far-right, but we will get to that shortly). In the Soviet Union (the USSR), throughout the 1920s, Stalin and the Soviet propaganda ministry successfully sold a bill of goods to many of their own people and the people in Europe and America, stating that communism was the way of the future. They issued reports, data, pictures, posters, and sponsored yet carefully escorted tours, which all showed that the USSR was making economic leaps and bounds. Much of it was false, but people wanted to fall for it, and so they did.

To prevent the fall of the German economy and nation and also to secure their reparations payments, the Allies began to slowly engage successive German governments with new, deferred, and milder ways to pay the war reparations. What follows is simple in the extreme, but it will help readers understand both how Germany slowly got on its feet in the later 1920s and one cause of the Great Depression of 1929.

The United States, which, while losing over 100,000 men in its short time in WWI, was not invaded, did not go through shortages, did not suffer economically (quite the contrary), and did not have the same hard feelings toward Germany that existed in Britain and France. From about 1916 onward, both Britain and France financed their war efforts and then turned around and bought weapons and supplies from the US. When WWI ended, the United States had become the strongest economy in the world, which sparked many cries of "war profiteering" and investigations in Congress.

Of all the combatants in the Great War, the US was the only nation not essentially flat broke, but people worried that the ripple effects of a European economic breakdown after the war would reach the shores of the United States. Therefore, over the course of a number of years and many discussions involving the Allies, most importantly, Germany and the United States (sometimes with the knowledge of the others and sometimes not), a system was put in place that would allow Germany to both pay back its debts and be able to invest in businesses to revive its economy. The United States would loan it the money to pay Britain and France at new interest rates. (After all, loaning money without interest just means you're out that particular sum of money, which you can't use for a period of time. Thus, interest is charged to make the loan worthwhile.) In turn, the British and French would use this money to pay back the United States for the loans they received during the war, which would then go back to Germany... Do you see how that works? It was an illusion, but it worked, at least for a while.

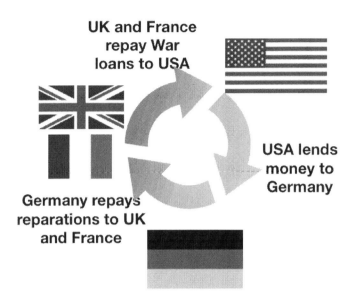

UK and France repay War loans to USA

USA lends money to Germany

Germany repays reparations to UK and France

Now, obviously, there were many other contributions to the Great Depression, but one of the least recognized was the cycle of payments pictured above. Hundreds of billions of dollars were taken out of circulation (therefore, they were not being used for investment, erosion control, public works, or for many of the other reasons for the Depression). This system worked until it didn't.

Still, from late 1923 onward, with fits and starts, the German economy began to improve. However, there is still one event of 1923 that we need to discuss, and it took place in Munich on November 9th, 1923. (Pay attention to the amazing recurrence of November 9th in German history as we go on. We have encountered one already—Kaiser Wilhelm II abdicated on November 9th.)

On November 9th, 1923, Adolf Hitler, accompanied by the famous General Erich Ludendorff; future German Air Force chief and first head of the Gestapo, Hermann Göring; and Ernst Röhm, future head of the SA, along with hundreds of followers, attempted to overthrow the government of Bavaria in the first step on a planned "March on Berlin" to overthrow the national government, similar to how Benito Mussolini had overthrown the Italian government in his famous "March on Rome" in October 1922.

Hitler's plan crumbled for various reasons, including cold feet on the part of some army officers and Bavarian politicians, poor planning, and an overestimation of his party's support. The famous Beer Hall Putsch (*putsch* is German for "coup") amounted to nothing, but Hitler's trial by right-wing judges (there was no jury system in Germany) gave the natural-born speaker a platform for announcing his resentment over the end of WWI, the Versailles Treaty, and the state of Germany. It was failure that propelled Hitler to success. His trial, the writing of his book *Mein Kampf* (*My Struggle*) while "incarcerated" in Landsberg Prison, and his decision to achieve power by legal means all stemmed from the failure of November 9th, 1923.

As a side note, Hitler's cell was essentially an apartment from which people and packages could go. It is well known that Hitler had a sweet tooth, so the people who visited him often brought chocolate or other sweets.

Illustration 24: Hitler in his "cell" at Landsberg with visitors for tea. His chauffeur, Emil Maurice, stands behind him.

Today, the days of the Weimar Republic are known almost as much for their artistic and cultural achievements and happenings as they are for the rise of Hitler and the Nazis. The years of relative stability (1924 to 1929) saw Germany, especially Berlin, become one of the cultural capitals of the Western world.

Why did this happen? In the years before the unification of Germany, when the country was a conglomeration of states and principalities, the laws and unspoken rules of censorship differed from area to area, but generally speaking, German artists, writers, and musicians were able to express themselves relatively freely. If they were not able to do so where they lived, they very often relocated, sometimes where laws governing expression were laxer, where the money was better, or both.

When Germany united in the latter part of the 19th century, things began to change, and several laws restricting expression were passed. With Wilhelm II's coming of age, the censorship of the government grew more profound, especially in regard to the written word, as it was much easier to censor than artistic works such as sculpture and painting. Remember that Wilhelm II was an absolute monarch at heart and a believer in the "divine right of kings" deep in his soul.

As a comparison, two periods of American history may further illustrate what happened in Germany under the Kaiser. Though both the 1920s and 1950s are famous for their rebellious groups (the flappers and bootleggers of the 1920s and the beatniks and motorcycle gangs of the 1950s), much of American society was a self-regulated, flat-top haircut culture of picket fences, cut lawns, cocktails parties, anti-communist witch hunts, and conformity. The famous American novel *Babbitt* by Sinclair Lewis (1922) portrays this life and culture perfectly. Though there were obvious differences (the worship of the military being one of them), German society during the Wilhelmine era was much the same.

As you have read, the end of WWI and the way it ended tore German society apart, and while artists of all kinds create even in the worst of times, the news and the events of the day drew people's attention far more than the latest painting or dance craze. Survival and political strife were the order of the day.

Once the occupation of the Ruhr and the hyperinflation had gotten under control, things began to settle down in Germany, at least on the surface. And as they did, life could get back to "normal"; only "normal," at least in Berlin and a couple of the other major cities, was a totally different thing than it had been.

One of the big changes that took place in the 1920s was the importation of American culture, especially jazz culture. This was truly the first time that American culture had invaded the shores of Europe, and making things even more foreign was the fact that many of the jazz artists coming to Europe (especially Paris and Berlin) were African American. They were leaving the United States for money and for a place to live and perform that was, for the most part, less discriminatory.

Berliners, as well as those in Hamburg (and yes, they are called "Hamburgers") and other cities, went crazy for American jazz, as well as the dance and fashion that went along with it. Naturally, many jazz fans were young city dwellers, but jazz made its way, in the form of radio and records, into smaller cities and larger towns as well. Not to be overlooked was the massive amount of drinking that went on at clubs and parties throughout Germany—again, Berlin was the most notorious. There was also a rise in drug use. Cocaine was legal, as it was in the United States as well, and heroin- and opium-based narcotics were easily available. The hundreds of thousands of wounded veterans were a ready customer base. Adding to that, pharmacists sold their drugs under the table for much more than they purchased them. Marijuana was relatively rare, but hashish from North Africa made its way to Berlin. This was "popular culture" for the masses, and it is well portrayed in the German TV program *Babylon Berlin*, which you can find on Netflix.

What a lot of people don't realize is that during the stable years of the Weimar Republic, the government funded the arts a great deal—far more than had ever been done throughout the Wilhelmine era. Though this funding was considerably lower on the budgetary totem pole, the thought behind it was sound: fund the arts and help return society to "normal."

Before we talk about the movies, paintings, plays, musicals, and novels of the Weimar era, we should also remember that, like other periods in other countries throughout history, the "golden age" of Weimar arts and culture came between two abysmally stagnant periods culturally. We've already spoken about the censorship and uniformity of Wilhelmine Germany, and obviously, what came after the Weimar era was far, far worse, so it should be no surprise that many people looked (and look) back at this period with fondness and nostalgia. And, of course, as people age, nostalgia grows.

Still, however, there is no question that what happened in Germany in the middle and late 1920s was a phenomenon, and while there were other centers of artistic achievement in Germany, Berlin became a magnet for people wanting to express themselves freely and to make money off those who did.

There are several reasons for the flowering of the arts in Germany during this time. Some have already been mentioned. Others include a terrific originality that took place in Berlin and spread outward to the rest of the Western world, and within this originality was the kind of eclectic mix of mediums, styles, and personalities that usually happen only once in a lifetime.

Berlin, being Germany's capital, had always drawn a variety of people despite being the center of an authoritarian regime. What's more, it was looked at as a "border city" between Western and

Eastern Europe, kind of like a frontier, and like most frontier cities, it drew a wild and creative crowd after the destruction of WWI.

In a sense, Berlin was the home of modern performance art. Warehouses, empty buildings, and vacant lots were all transformed into theaters of one sort or another. One of the many themes, not only of the performance art and street theater of the time but also in movies and books, was technology. Remember, WWI was the first mass-produced war and brought not only machine guns but also submarines, airplanes, tanks, and the radio to the fore. Many of Berlin's performances during this time were about how technology was changing life and how small and inconsequential human beings were becoming in the face of these new technologies. Perhaps the most famous and long lasting of these examples is the film *Metropolis* (1927) by Fritz Lang.

Berlin also became the center of European filmmaking during this period, and the studio at Babelsberg outside Berlin was one of the largest in the world. It still produces movies (Quentin Tarantino insisted his *Inglorious Basterds*, with its WWII theme, be filmed there). While movies such as *Blue Angel*, *The Cabinet of Dr. Caligari*, and *M* were controversial and worldwide phenomena (and launched the international careers of Marlene Dietrich and Peter Lorre, to name just two), just as many bad films were made, with many of them trying to make money off youth culture and the Jazz Age.

Jazz wasn't the only music being made in the Weimar years. Most famously, the musical *The Threepenny Opera* became the first German musical, and it was a hit overseas as well, especially with its depiction of street life in Germany.

Classical music moved away from the works of the 1800s and into new territory as well. The most famous German composer of the time was Arnold Strindberg, whose works exploring atonality were a unique investigation into the construction of music. However, all but the most serious of musicians found it remote, dreary, and uninspiring. Music, too, seemed to reflect a new age of technology.

Architecture did as well, and perhaps the most famous school of architectural design during this time was Bauhaus (literally "House for the Building Arts"). Bauhaus not only considered architecture in the design of its buildings but also function and, to a degree, useful style. Walter Gropius, Ludwig Mies van der Rohe, and other architects consulted with artists in other mediums, such as Paul Klee and Wassily Kandinsky, to create a new style that walked a line between function and form. Many of their buildings also reflect the effect technology had on the thinking of the time.

Of course, not everyone in Berlin was an artist, writer, musician, or sculptor. Most people in Berlin were housewives, workers, fathers, or wounded vets begging for pennies—in other words, they were regular people. Some of them embraced the changes, while some did not. Still, others were spectators of a sort, as there always are in situations like that—for example, most of the "hippies" that lived in San Francisco in the late 1960s and early 1970s arrived long after the "hey-day" of the "Summer of Love" of 1967.

Still, being in Berlin in the mid-1920s must have been something to behold, especially for the young. One of the things the period is most famous for is the experimentation with sexuality and gender, which went on in public at the clubs and behind closed doors (sometimes at those same clubs!) Though there was much experimentation going on, especially in Berlin, it was never as widespread as the media and politicians (then and now) made it out to be, but it made great headlines and salacious secret reading.

For reasons that sociologists are still trying to explain, Berlin (along with Paris) became a hub for sexual experimentation in the 1920s. Some of it was likely due to the idea of still being alive after the war, hyperinflation, and civil unrest, among other things. Much of it was likely due to the liberal atmosphere generated in the theaters, clubs, and dance halls. Whatever the cause, Berlin became infamous as a place where "anything went." The movie *Cabaret* (1972), based on the book *Goodbye to Berlin* (1939), portrays the time and the feeling extremely well.

In 1968, US presidential candidate Richard Nixon proclaimed that Americans of the "silent majority" would vote for him and stand up for "traditional American values," as opposed to the "free love" and drugs the hippies practiced and used (which were never as widespread as the media and Nixon made them out to be). Way before Nixon's call for the "silent majority" to rise up and take America back from the hippies, a wide spectrum of political parties (mostly on the right but some on the left as well) were condemning Weimar culture and the changes seemingly taking over German life.

Though the nightclubs and cabarets of the 1920s went on into the 1930s, the onset of the Great Depression in October 1929 put a serious damper on the celebratory lifestyle of Weimar Germany and especially that of Berlin. What was to come was more hunger, unemployment, political strife, and violence, resulting in a regime that would put an end to almost every aspect of Weimar culture within six months of it taking power.

Illustration 25: Cabaret poster of the 1920s: "Berlin, the city of beautiful women," a comic opera. The bear is the symbol of the city of Berlin, as are the flags.

Illustration 26: "Our last hope."

Chapter 7 – Hitler, Anti-Semitism, and the Rise of the Nazis

This e-book is an introduction to the history of Germany from 1870 to the present day. Perhaps you purchased it for yourself because you felt there were some gaps in your knowledge or as a gift to a young person who is tackling the subject at school. If you're one of the people who are familiar with Hitler and the rise of the Nazis and WWII, you're likely to be familiar with much or all that follows in this chapter. However, since these books are written as introductory guides and since learning about this time period is of the utmost importance, we are going to start at the beginning and cover the entire horrible period in as much detail as possible.

Hitler was born in Austria in 1889 in the small town of Braunau am Inn. His father, Alois, was twenty-three years older than his third wife and Hitler's mother, Klara, who was also Alois's first cousin once-removed on his mother's side. It is not known who Alois's father was, which haunted the anti-Semitic Adolf in later life with thoughts that he might possibly be of partial Jewish heritage. Hitler had five brothers and one sister. Only his sister Paula lived into adulthood, dying in 1960. Hitler did have a stepsister, Angela, the daughter of his father's second wife. Angela's daughter, Geli, Hitler's niece, was Adolf's first and perhaps only true love other than his mother. She died by her own hand in 1931, most likely due to the oppressive nature of her relationship with Hitler, who, by that time, was a national figure.

By all accounts, Alois Hitler was the typical Austrian/German father of his age, perhaps even more so. He was an authoritarian father who beat his wife and children, and Adolf seems to have seen his mother as both protector and someone to protect as he got older. Volumes of psychological studies have been written to determine if Hitler's childhood was the main factor in what he later became.

What we do know is that Hitler was utterly devoted to his mother, and following the death of his father in 1903, Klara moved to the small provincial city of Linz with her two children. By 1907, Hitler had moved to Vienna to study art, but he was recalled to Linz because his mother had been diagnosed with breast cancer. After a long battle, a mastectomy, and a primitive and painful form of chemotherapy, she died at home with her family. An interesting facet to this story is that the family doctor, Eduard Bloch, was Jewish. By all accounts, Hitler liked and respected Bloch. Later in life, Bloch reported that he had never seen someone so devastated by a death as Hitler was by his mother's. Later on, Hitler allowed Bloch and his wife to flee Austria without trouble during the Nazis' persecution of the Jews after Germany's union with Austria in 1938.

With the death of his mother, Hitler returned to Vienna, living off his portion of his father's civil servant pension and the watercolor postcards he sold on the streets of the Austro-Hungarian capital. For many years, it was believed that Hitler lived in abject poverty in Vienna (this largely came from his own account of that time), but while he surely did not live a life of luxury or even a lower-middle-class existence, he was not destitute as he portrayed.

Nonetheless, it was not an easy existence, and for much of his time in Vienna, he lived in what used to be called a dosshouse but now would be referred to as a cheap men-only motel for the relatively down-and-out.

What most residents of the places where Hitler lived remembered were his sudden rantings. He was normally a quiet man who kept to himself or kept company with his friend from Linz, August Kubizek, who shared a similar history, having lost both parents. Suddenly, though, Hitler would stand up and begin ranting about art or the lack of cultural awareness among his fellows. And after having spent some time in Vienna, he began ranting about politics and the Jews.

Hitler was not without artistic talent. He likely could have pursued a career as an illustrator for an architectural or real estate company or perhaps illustrated books or magazines. That was not for Hitler, though. Around this point in his life, he seemed to develop the megalomania that would both raise him to world power and lower him into madness. Hitler fancied himself a "fine artist" in the vein of Michelangelo, Titian, Rembrandt, and others. Even the most inexperienced eye could tell he did not have that type of talent, but few do.

Hitler twice submitted his work for admission to the highly esteemed Vienna Academy of Art and was rejected both times. The rejections noted Hitler's ability to render buildings and scenery adequately, but his attempts at recreating the human form were elemental and without feeling. At this time, Hitler was also rejected from the Vienna School of Architecture for the bureaucratic reason of not being able to provide a secondary school diploma from Linz.

These failed attempts to achieve what he had long dreamed seems to have been one of the foundational points for Hitler's transformation from a relatively quiet, apolitical street artist into a man fixated on both politics and one of the cultural trends of the time, at least in Germany and Austria: the "science" of race.

However, in actuality, race was not an issue limited to Germany and Austria. In much of Western Europe and the United States, segments of the dominant population and the upper classes began to ask themselves why it seemed that the white European nationalities had come to dominate much of the world by that time. They were also on their way toward dominating what was left, including China.

The idea of superiority was not limited to Europeans. The Chinese had called themselves the Middle Kingdom for millennia, as it was the kingdom around which the rest of the world revolved and which was due respect and tribute. There were segments, rather large segments, of people in Muslim/Ottoman lands that had felt the same way, and though much of that belief was centered around religion, the subject peoples of the Arabic Mohammedan Empire in the late 8th century until the 12th century would tell you that it was clear that the Arabs felt themselves superior to many of the people they had conquered, including those in parts of Spain. There are other examples throughout history outside of Europe, and it continues to happen today.

What makes the European notion of supremacy, which began in earnest in the late 1800s onward, different and notable is that it was coupled with both military might and "science." By the start of World War One, much of the globe was either overlorded or heavily influenced by Western countries. This was due to the rich natural resources; high population density, with its accompanying rapid exchange of ideas; the rise of the centrally governed nation state throughout Europe and its high level of organization; and its weapons. Vast distances, climate, topography, and tribal warfare contributed to the comparative weakness of much of the rest of the world in the late 19th century.

One exception was Japan, which had united in the early 1600s. The Japanese refused to let Westerners into all but one or two cities for centuries, and it was also relatively small and isolated. With the arrival of the Americans under Matthew Perry in the early 1850s, Japan was forced to open to the world for trade, but they did so wisely, limiting Western contact and setting the Westerners against each other. In the early 1870s, Japan rejected its feudal system and set about developing a modern economy with an emperor at the head of a parliamentary government led by aristocrats and industrialists. In the late 1890s and in 1905, Japan shockingly and convincing defeated China and Russia in two wars and set itself upon a course of imperial expansion that would lead to WWII in the Pacific. Not far under the surface of Japan's expansion was the notion of the superiority and "purity" of the Japanese race. Late 19th-century/early 20th-century Japan is the most convincing example outside of Europe of both the tendency of humans to set themselves above others and the desire to conquer them.

However, while the Japanese could point to the ancient and supposedly divine nature of their imperial family, the Europeans used the evidence of their military might and Darwin's theory of evolution and its accompanying notion of the "survival of the fittest."

Simply and concisely, among much of the literate population of Europe, the idea that human beings were both part of and the apex of the natural world began to spread, and within that belief, the idea caught on that, similar to what happens in nature, those who were stronger and adaptable survived and thrived. Those who did not died out or were killed. That was the rationale behind white supremacy of the time.

What historians, anthropologists, sociologists, and psychologists have found since the time of Hitler is that, generally speaking, the ideas of racial supremacy start or reignite among segments at the top of society and from the lower middle class downward. The reasoning behind the first is relatively obvious. Among the latter is the idea of being part of something more powerful than just oneself and one's "poorer and less powerful" situation. As Hitler's popularity grew, many in the middle class, especially in the countryside and villages, became attracted to the philosophy of German (or white) supremacy.

Another group to which these beliefs often appeal are younger males, who frequently feel controlled by and/or are at the whim of others, and you can easily create a hostile young man (and, in more recent times, women) who believes the world is against him.

Hitler was not the first to spell out these beliefs, though he wrote about them considerably in his book. The French aristocratic theorist Comte ("Count") de Gobineau (1816-1882) began writing extensively on the ideas of white supremacy combined with evolutionary theory in the latter part of the 19th century. It was Gobineau that incorrectly applied the word "Aryan" to the Germanic peoples of northern Europe.

Alongside Gobineau in influence was Houston Stewart Chamberlain (1855-1927), an upper-class Englishman who later settled in Germany and wrote in German. Chamberlain was the epitome of the rebellious loner, just as Hitler became, and for that reason, among others, he was a favorite of Hitler's. In 1899, Chamberlain's German-language book *Die Grundlagen des neunzehnten Jahrhunderts* (*The Foundations of the 19th Century*) became one of the foundational stones of "scientific" white supremacy that became popular at the time, especially in German and Austria. The science of Chamberlain's book was really opinion dressed up in scientific and philosophical language without any scientific evidence or fieldwork of any kind.

Both Gobineau and Chamberlain used the term "Aryan" to describe the Germanic "races" of Europe. (Today, science only recognizes three or four "races" of human beings, and even that is done hesitantly. "Ethnicity" is more often used today.) According to Gobineau and Chamberlain, Aryans were groups of very ancient peoples (some white supremacists of the time had them occupying the mythical island of Atlantis) who had supplied the foundational stones of the great civilizations of the past, such as Greece, Rome, and Persia. In fact, it is from the latter that we get the actual term "Aryan"; the word was used as a descriptor for groups of people who lived in the area of Persia (modern-day Iran) to northern India.

Gobineau and those who followed him believed that the ancient Aryans were tall, athletic, blond, and blue-eyed and that the original "bloodline" of the ancient Aryans had survived in northern Europe but had faded out in the Middle East and India due to interbreeding with "lower" races, specifically the Semitic peoples, which include Arabs but primarily refers to the Jews. Again, all of this was based not only on wishful thinking but also on appearances—none of this was based on any kind of scientific study or data.

Hitler latched onto the ideas of Gobineau and especially Chamberlain. He also took their ideas and combined them with others, which were espoused by two figures who influenced him more directly and emotionally—Vienna's mayor at the time of Hitler's residency there, Karl Lueger, a vicious anti-Semite, and the famed composer Richard Wagner, whose operas elevated Germanic heroes above the lower "races" of German and Nordic mythology and who was a notorious anti-Semite. (Interestingly, Houston Stewart Chamberlain's life and outlook were said to also have been changed by Wagner's music and operas, and later in life, he married Wagner's daughter, Eva).

Lueger's anti-Semitism was loud, crude, and political. He railed against Jews as a "foreign element." In Vienna and Austria of the time, most Austrian Jews were highly assimilated into society, as they were in Germany. They generally kept to themselves but obviously practiced their religious beliefs, though an increasing number of German and Austrian Jews were becoming less observant. However, to Lueger and others, the Jews in Austria were symbolized by those who had come to Vienna from the eastern parts of the Austro-Hungarian Empire. This population was more observant and much more visible, wearing traditional clothing and hairstyles, especially among the men. This helped to set them apart. Hitler appears to have begun developing truly virulent anti-Semitic opinions after being in Vienna for some time and consuming Lueger's speeches and writings, along with those of the mayor's political allies.

Before we continue with the story of Hitler's life before his rise to power, we should make an attempt to explain why anti-Semitism exists in the first place. To begin with, please remember that this e-book is an introduction to German history and that, unfortunately, anti-Semitism in that country led to the Holocaust. In simplifying the roots of anti-Semitism, please know that we understand the topic is both deep and emotional, but for our purposes here, we are going to limit our discussion of the topic to a very basic explanation, with which you may or may not fully agree with but which summarizes the knowledge of many historians who are experts on the topic.

Anti-Semitism has six basic historical foundations that go back to the time of the Roman Empire. Rome has two distinct periods: the Roman Republic (509 BCE–27 BCE) and the Roman Empire (27 BCE–c. 410 CE). What's confusing is that Rome began its conquests, the building of its *empire*, under the Roman Republic.

First, when the Romans expanded into the area that today encompasses Israel, they encountered something they had never experienced before: a monotheistic culture—one that worships a single deity. Virtually all of the other cultures conquered by or assimilated into the Roman Empire were polytheistic like the Romans, meaning they worshiped many gods that resembled the Romans pantheon in all but name.

Three problems arose from this. Firstly, the Romans and Jews fundamentally did not understand each other's views of the world and the universe. The Jews insisted that the Roman gods were false and vice versa. When Rome was eventually ruled by an emperor, beginning with Augustus, the state insisted that the people it dominated essentially had to worship the emperor as a god, whether this emperor was dead and alive. This was something the Jews would categorically not do.

During Jesus Christ's lifetime, tensions between the Jews and Romans were high, with occasional uprisings and frequent riots against Roman rule occurring. The Romans had traditionally adopted a "divide and conquer" strategy in the formation of their far-flung empire, and, to a degree, the clash of ideas between Christ and his followers and the Jewish establishment suited the Romans very well until it threatened to get out of hand.

You likely know the story. Jesus was accused by the Jewish authorities of claiming he was the Messiah, the savior of the world, and the Son of God. This both went against contemporary Jewish teaching and threatened the "powers that be" among both the Romans and the Jews. At his "trial," Jesus was offered up to the Jewish crowd by the Roman governor of Judea, Pontius Pilate. Pilate offered the crowd two men, one of whom would go free and the other who would be crucified: Jesus and the accused murderer Barabbas. Threatened by Jesus's supposed heresy, the crowd demanded that he be crucified and that Barabbas go free. You know the rest of the story.

However, as Christianity became the dominant religion of the later Roman Empire and the Early Middle Ages after the Western Roman Empire's fall, the Jews came to be blamed for the death of Christ. This idea was combined with new myths surrounding the Jews, becoming a deadly fallacy. In an age of great faith in religious leaders and illiteracy, these ideas became almost a required belief, especially as Jews believed that the Messiah was still to come, which enraged Christians, who saw this as denial of Christ's divinity.

This Jewish "blood guilt," as it came to be called, makes as much sense as blaming a white farmer in 21st-century Iowa for the genocidal wars against the Native Americans in the 18th and 19th

centuries. Still, ignorance, combined with beliefs backed by authority figures, can be powerful.

The bubonic plague (known as the Black Plague or the Black Death) struck Europe with a vengeance in the mid-1340s to the 1350s. Some estimates have the death toll at nearly 25 percent of Europe's population, but the plague (along with other deadly diseases, the most prevalent of which was smallpox) struck with alarming frequency until relatively modern times.

The idea that the plague was spread by rodents, or rather the germs in the fleas, which then fed on the blood of infected rodents, was relatively unknown, though some did have the notion that somehow fleas and rodents were responsible. What people did not know with certainty until the mid-1800s was that disease was spread by germs. They believed it was spread by bad air, bad water, perhaps bad blood, and pus, but they did not realize it was something one could not see, like germs.

In the Middle Ages, due to the reasons explained above and others, Jews were frequently required to live separately from the rest of the population. When they weren't required to do so, they often did so voluntarily for safety. As a result, it seemed to many that the Jews did not get the plague, or at least not as often. Again, you must remember, this was a time of profound ignorance and illiteracy. So, when people asked themselves, "Why don't the Jews get the plague or suffer from it as bad as everyone else?" they came to the conclusion that the Jews had started it. Simple as that. They started it, were immune from it, and were spreading it to the rest of the population as revenge or at Satan's command.

The Jews, of course, got the plague as well. They simply may have died at a lesser rate simply because the people who blamed them for it forced them to live apart, therefore making them more protected from the spread of germs.

In addition to the "blood libel" of Jesus's death and the plague, other myths around the Jews arose. When something is separate and alien, and especially when the observer is uneducated, gaps in knowledge are replaced by supposition, superstition, and fear. Along with the above, Jews were frequently accused of witchcraft and holding human sacrifices. A popular myth talked of Jews kidnapping Christian virgins, cutting their throats, and using their blood in their unleavened matzoh bread.

And as if this wasn't bad enough, other edicts from the Catholic Church indirectly made life worse for European Jews. The most notable for our purposes here were the laws against usury, the loaning of money for interest.

Usury was seen as "un-Christian," as people believed it took advantage of those who were in a worse economic position. Since interest rates were not set, they were essentially whatever the lender decided he could get, and the more desperate a person or business was, the higher the interest rate. It was also seen as slothful since one made money but did nothing to earn it.

Now, if someone came to you and asked you for a 100,000-dollar loan and you didn't charge interest, what would happen? First, you would not be able to use that money yourself for investments or whatever for however long it took for the person to pay you back. Second, inflation makes money worth less over time, so the 100,000 dollars that you lent (without interest) might be worth only 80,000 when you got it back, so in the end, you lose money if interest isn't charged. Interest makes a modern economy function.

Since Christians were forbidden to lend money at interest and since everyone in Europe, except the Jews, was subject to these laws (though, of course, many Christians violated these edicts), who would one go to for money when no one else would lend it to you because it was a losing proposition? The Jews. And we know what frequently happens to relationships between people who loan money—resentment.

Making this worse, many people would take loans from Jewish lenders and skip the agreed payments or simply not pay at all. When this happened, the Jewish lender would often be powerless to collect. As a result, interest rates rose (as did resentment), and Jews complained to the authorities, who oftentimes saw the Jews as "money-grubbers" whose sole concern was profit. Jews also went into the pawnbroker business, which is essentially another form of loans at interest. By doing so, it caused them to be viewed as taking advantage of poor Christians.

As time went by, several Jewish families in Europe became large banking interests, the most famous of which were the Rothschilds, who are still a favorite target of white supremacists and conspiracy theorists today. Of course, many non-Jewish families became bankers too, but they were often viewed in a different light.

Outside of their own settlements, in much of Europe, Jews were forbidden to engage in certain trades. For much of the Middle Ages, guilds, organizations of specific trades, such as woodworkers, saddlers, bakers, or painters, to name a few, dominated small businesses in Europe. It was in the interest of these guilds to limit competition, and one way this was done was by passing laws that restricted what professions Jews could participate in.

This forced many Jews, especially in the cities, to go into areas that were not forbidden to them. We've already mentioned banking. Law, administration, the arts, writing, and acting as middlemen between the guilds and the general public were not forbidden. In Germany, in 1933, when Hitler came to power, the Jews represented about 1 percent of the population: seven hundred thousand out of seventy million. In most other parts of Europe, the ratio was about the same, with Eastern Europe, especially Poland and Russia, being on the higher end (and both countries endured far more vicious anti-Semitism for most of European history until WWII, something of which the Nazis took full advantage).

Of course, most Jews were poor and were persecuted frequently. However, in the cities where there were more opportunities, Jews were seen as having massive influence compared to their proportion of the population, and the ironic thing was that much of this perceived influence was caused by laws or customs created by the Europeans themselves.

In the early 20th century, anti-Semites added communism to the long list of things for which to blame Jews, as Karl Marx was a Jew, as well as a number of leading communists in the Soviet Union (though they were still a minority). Oddly enough, the Nazis also blamed the Jews for "greedy capitalism," which is the exact opposite of communism.

It was thought that the Jews, as they supported the ultra-capitalists and communists, were trying to rule the world from the shadows. This was "proven" with the publication of the so-called *Protocols of the Elders of Zion* in the early 20th century, which claimed to be the transcripts and ideas of leading Jews planning to take over the world. The work is a piece of fiction, and it was called out as such by most at the time. It clearly lifts sentiments and literal paragraphs from a number of earlier published works published. Still, in nations and areas that had historically experienced anti-Semitism, including the United States, where half a million copies were paid for by Henry Ford, a notorious anti-Semite, the *Protocols* seemed real enough and seemed to confirm their already long-held beliefs.

With the advent of what came to be known as social Darwinism, the idea that certain "races" were superior to others and that "only the strong survived" caused the persecution of the Jews to go beyond religious persecution. This pseudo-science declared that Judaism was not just a religion but a "part of the blood." German families with Jewish last names, even if they had converted to Christianity decades, perhaps even a century or so before the rise of

Hitler, were not safe. To Hitler and others at the time, "Jewishness," as well as "German-ness," was biological, not something you could discard by converting.

Like any prejudice, most anti-Semites could not even begin to tell you the historical causes behind their anti-Semitism. It was simply passed down from generation to generation, friend to friend, neighbor to neighbor, and it was made worse by both the occasional mention of certain ideas (like the idea that their Jewish neighbor in Poland might somehow be responsible for the death of Christ) and events (like the Great Depression). That's the thing about hate, though; it doesn't have to be logical. It just has to make you feel better than someone else. And since hate does not require logic, reason, or facts to exist, it is difficult to counter and easy to spread.

Illustration 27: Nazi poster for their film The Eternal Jew, *which compared disease-carrying hordes of rats to Germany's Jewish population. The poster depicts the infamous caricature of an Eastern European Jew holding out money with one hand and a whip in the other while holding a map of Germany stamped with the symbol of communism.*

World War I for Hitler

By 1914, Hitler, an Austrian, was a confirmed anti-Semite and began to adhere to the popular ideas of German/Nordic superiority. Because the Austro-Hungarian Empire consisted of a mélange of different ethnic groups, and because he perceived Germany as being stronger, Hitler evaded the Austrian draft and crossed the border into Bavaria when war threatened to erupt. He joined the German Army when war was declared. A famous picture of Hitler in Munich cheering the war news is most likely a fake (it was later serendipitously "discovered" to be taken by the man who later became Hitler's official photographer, Heinrich Hoffmann), but we can assume, both by Hitler's own writings and speeches and the general mood of the country in August 1914, that he did indeed cheer the outbreak of the war.

Hitler served in the 16th Bavarian Reserve Infantry Regiment throughout the war. He served on or near the front lines on the Western Front. His primary job throughout the conflict was that of messenger, running information from the rear trenches to the front. By all accounts, he served dutifully and bravely, earning the Iron Cross Second Class in 1914 and the Iron Cross First Class in 1918. Ironically, the officer who recommended the latter was Lieutenant Hugo Gutmann, who was Jewish. Hitler had also been wounded by shellfire in 1916, but he returned to the front before he was due to.

Illustration 28: Corporal Hitler (left), the day he was awarded the Iron Cross First Class.

In October 1918, Hitler was a victim of a British gas attack, which left his eyes highly irritated. In the years since the war, studies of contemporary accounts of his and other cases from the time attribute Hitler's end-of-the-war blindness to hysteria; in other words, he had reached his breaking point. Still, for all intents and purposes, he was blind. When the news of the armistice and Germany's seeming surrender reached him at the convalescent hospital in northeastern Germany, Hitler reported that upon hearing the news, his sight came back, and he felt "destined" to lead Germany from the hard times he was sure would come. The event was longer and more drawn-out than what Hitler portrayed, but the crux is that Hitler seemingly went from rejected artist to a man who had convinced himself that somehow "providence" had singled him out for a great destiny.

After returning to Munich once the war ended, Hitler was one of the few Germans who remained in the army. In 1919, he was tasked with keeping an eye on several far-right political parties emerging in the violent aftermath of WWI in Bavaria. One of these groups was the DAP (*Deutsche Arbeiterpartei* or "German Workers' Party"). After attending a number of their meetings and frequenting the beer hall where they gathered, Hitler realized that the DAP espoused many of the same beliefs that he had developed, such as his hatred of the Versailles Treaty and its many restrictions, German superiority, the need for Germany to gain "living space" (*Lebensraum*) in Eastern Europe and Russia for its densely populated country, and the notion that the German Army, especially its *Frontsoldaten* or "front line soldiers," had been "stabbed in the back" by the SPD and the Jews.

As 1919 rolled into 1920, Hitler began to make speeches to party members and those curious about the party in various right-wing hangouts in Munich. Almost immediately, Hitler and his comrades within the party realized that he possessed an extraordinary talent for speaking. On February 24th, 1920, Hitler and the DAP held a meeting that two thousand people attended. Hitler's speech, which described the twenty-five-point platform of the party that he and two others had written, and its reception solidified his place as one of the DAP's leaders. In March 1920, he was discharged from the army and then worked full-time for the party.

By 1920, Hitler had become one of the leaders of the DAP. In 1921, by virtue of his speaking ability, which was beginning to draw large crowds in Munich, Hitler became the leader of the party, which changed its name from *Deutsche Arbeiterpartei* to *Nationalsozialistische Deutsche Arbeiterpartei* (also known as the National Socialist German Workers' Party, the NSDAP, or the Nazi Party).

The name change reflected a desire by its leadership to set it apart from other right-wing parties and the political left, which frequently used the word "workers" to highlight their adherence to socialism or communism. In the case of the NSDAP, aspects of socialism were mixed with intense nationalism, as opposed to the communists' ideas of the universal brotherhood of the workers.

By late 1921, Hitler, recognizing his own speaking (and therefore recruiting) capability, as well facing down a mutiny within the party, had become the absolute undisputed leader of the NSDAP. Alongside Hitler, as he moved his way toward becoming the unquestioned leader of the Nazis, was Ernst Röhm, an army captain who became the commander of the party's paramilitary, the *Sturmabteilung* or SA. Hermann Göring, the successor to Manfred von Richthofen's squadron in WWI, also became attracted to the movement and Hitler. Göring was a nationally recognized figure due to his role in WWI. By the 1920s, Munich had become a magnet for extreme right-wing politicians and believers. Among them was Rudolf Hess, a WWI veteran who had spent much of his youth in Egypt and developed a profound dislike for anyone who was not white, as well as Heinrich Himmler, a young man who had just missed action in WWI to his utter regret. Hess was to become Hitler's deputy and transcriber of *Mein Kampf,* while Heinrich Himmler became the head of Hitler's protection detachment or *Schutzstaffel,* a section of the SA better known as the SS.

One of Hitler's more important early supporters was General Erich Ludendorff of WWI fame, who was a central figure in right-wing politics in Munich after the war. It was Ludendorff that supposedly lent "legitimacy" to the Nazis' Beer Hall Putsch of 1923. This coup attempt ended in utter failure, but Hitler's testimony in court, which was really speeches permitted by the presiding judges, made him a national figure, as his "speeches" were reported in the national papers. However, while Hitler did garner national attention, most Germans regarded him as more of a political oddity, as a person who would soon pass from the political scene than any kind of real politician.

When Hitler was released from Landsberg Prison in late 1924, the NSDAP was in disarray. For much of 1925 and 1926, Hitler worked to rebuild the party and make it a national presence. The experience of 1923 had taught him that a small local revolt would hardly succeed in propelling the Nazis to national power. He determined that the Nazis' road to national power was going to be determined at the ballot box, so, along with his followers, he set about creating a national organization that would be represented in every German state, city, town, and village. It was at this point that Hitler became the unquestioned leader of the party and began to be addressed as *Führer* ("leader").

In 1924, a small man with decidedly dark "un-Aryan" features, a club foot, and a noticeable limp joined the party, and within a short time, he became the leader of the NSDAP in Berlin, a notoriously leftist city. This was Dr. Josef Goebbels, who had studied language and language history in Heidelberg and who was rapidly becoming a master of propaganda. Nazi propaganda depicted Hitler and the NSDAP as vigorous, powerful, and dedicated to Germany and its people (especially the "forgotten man" at the bottom of society). Conversely, the Nazis' opponents were portrayed as out of touch, old, corrupt, uncaring, and arrogant. Of course, much of the NSDAP's propaganda was aimed at the Jews and communists, who were often considered one and the same, and "helping" the German population understand that they were the main source of the nation's woes.

From 1924 to 1929, the Nazis built a highly efficient organization. However, as things began to become more stable within the Weimar Republic, party membership grew relatively slowly, though the Nazis did have a national presence and did elect its members to both state legislatures and the Reichstag, the national parliament, though in relatively small numbers.

It took the Great Depression to propel Hitler and the Nazis to national power.

Chapter 8 – The Nazis Take Power

Throughout the 1920s, the Nazis grew in membership. In 1925, there were just under 30,000 members. In 1929, there were nearly 110,000. This does not account for the number of people who worked for or supported the Nazis and were not official party members, which was probably underestimated at the time, both from the nature of early scientific polling and the reluctance of many "respectable" Germans to be openly identified with the NSDAP.

Despite the growth in their members and despite considerable work in organization, the NSDAP, while somewhat strong in conservative German states like Bavaria, was not able to pull more than 3 percent of the vote for the Reichstag. They did particularly poorly in the cities, and while they had already made their presence known in the countryside, villages, and towns, they made a bigger push in these areas for future elections. Though the population of Germany had changed considerably from the time of Bismarck and industrialization, most Germans still lived in rural areas or in small towns and villages.

Within both the cities and without, the Nazis increased their support by forming wings that were designed to appeal to specific demographic groups. You likely know of the Hitler Youth (*Hitlerjugend* in German), which appealed to young and teenage boys as a vital and strong alternative to the Boy Scouts and other youth groups that existed throughout Germany. Of course, the constant indoctrination and propaganda aimed at the youth helped their movement. These young men or boys, especially when their families were going through tough times or when their parents just didn't understand them, appreciated someone telling them not only that they were worthy people but that they were worthy of conquering the world.

Alongside the Hitler Youth, which was male-only, was the **BDM** or *Bund Deutsche Mädel* (the "League of German Maidens" or the "Band of German Maidens"). (As a side note, many times you'll see this translated as the "League of German Girls," which is incorrect. "Maidens" was used purposely to convey both purity and hearken back to another time, a supposed "German Golden Age."). The BDM did encourage girls to take up athletics, as you will see in many propaganda films, but it also stressed domestic life and child-rearing. In the Nazi worldview (or *Weltanschauung*, a word you can frequently see in Nazi speeches, as well as modern history books about the period), a woman's place was in the home, raising large numbers of children to help the Germans conquer and colonize the world. Before the Nazis took power, and more quietly afterward, many non-Nazis, especially more "proper" young women, came up with a nickname for the BDM: *Bund Deutsche Matratze* or "League of German Mattresses," as it was well known, and has since been proven with data from the period, that the number of pregnancies among girls and young women increased after Nazi Party and youth rallies.

Illustration 29: A German student propaganda poster. "The German student fights for Führer and People." The flag and uniform are that of the Hitler Youth.

Illustration 30: Poster for the League of German Maidens.

As you can plainly see, the Nazis' obsession with blond-haired, blue-eyed "perfection" is very evident.

The Nazis penetrated many segments of German society, from lawyers to farmers to teachers. As times got worse in 1929, these groups and the German public at large kept beating the same drum. "See what the November criminals, the Versailles Treaty, the Allies, the communists, and the Jews have done to Germany?" "Germans have lost everything." "The people are begging in the streets. The people have no dignity. No honor." "Hitler will restore Germany's strength, honor, and dignity!" Just right there, you essentially have a synopsis of every speech made by Hitler and his minions from 1929 until they came to power in 1933.

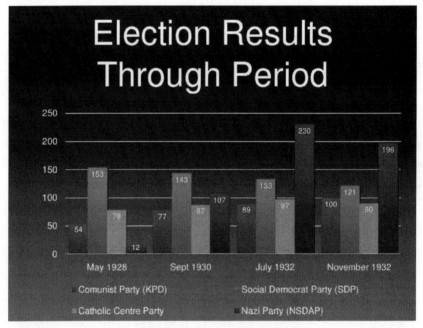

As you can see from the chart above, the Nazis gained ninety-five seats in the Reichstag after the crash of 1929. The Communists also gained seats, but while their gains came almost exclusively from the cities, the Nazis' base after 1929 was broader. Add to that the notion that the other major and some of the minor parties would gather against the Communists when needed.

In 1925, Field Marshal Paul von Hindenburg was elected president. He was seen as a strong figure, and the conservative parties and interests in Germany believed they could count on him to keep the extremists in line. This primarily meant the Communist Party, but before 1929, it also meant the Nazis.

However, after 1929, the nature of German politics changed. Many people believe that things changed toward dictatorship only after Hitler took power. This is incorrect. From 1929 onward, conservatives in both the Centre Party and those allied with the military became the chancellor. Each of them—Heinrich Brüning, Franz von Papen, and Kurt von Schleicher—ruled for short periods of time: two years and two months 169 days, and 56 days, respectively).

What these men all had in common was a hatred of liberal democracy, communists, the Social Democrats, and disorder. To varying degrees, they each wanted a return to the monarchy or perhaps a dictatorship with Hindenburg as its figurehead. None of them was willing to nor had the support to take direct action to make this happen, but from 1929 to 1932, each of them made important changes to the German political landscape, which helped Hitler establish his dictatorship when he came to power.

As you can see from the chart above, the Nazis gained the most votes in the election of July 1932. In addition to taking advantage of the bad times that had beset Germany and the world, Hitler and the Nazis also employed modern techniques in their election efforts. They made a point to seem decisive, a party of action and movement. At the top was Hitler, who seemed to appear all over Germany, almost at the same time. Hitler was the first politician to make use of the plane as a campaign tool, flying thousands of miles during election cycles and appearing in cities from north to south, sometimes on the same day. By the time Hitler took power, he and Josef Goebbels had become masters of political propaganda.

Throughout the 1920s, the SA had fought street battles with paramilitary groups of other parties, primarily that of the Communists. It was not just political opposition that the SA went after; of course, Jews and those who dressed in more modern Jazz Age type clothes and wore their hair longer were also targets of increasing levels of street violence during the Depression. For a time, the SA was banned, but as times got worse and as the Nazis gained more power, the traditional conservatives believed they could use the Nazis and their thugs against their own political opponents. However, the SA, whose leader, Ernst Röhm, made no secret of his wish of replacing the army with his SA, which, by the mid-1920s, numbered 400,000 men (after Hitler became chancellor, this number increased to over *two million*). This last notion, combined with Röhm's not-so-secret homosexuality and his leaning toward a more radical socialism than Hitler, made the army uneasy, but they were still hesitant to throw their support behind Hitler. This would change in 1934.

In July 1932, the Nazis became the largest party in the Reichstag, but another election was called that November. In this election, Hitler and the Nazis lost votes, and many historians believe that they might have continued on a downward spiral if events had played out a bit differently. The NSDAP was practically broke from the repeated state and national elections that took place at the time, which was due to both scheduling and no-confidence/coalition voting. The economy had begun to show small signs of improvement, and the people were tired of the street violence taking place every day, especially in the cities.

Hitler had asked or put out feelers for President Hindenburg to name him chancellor: once in July, when his popularity was greatest, and again in November, when the Nazis still held a considerable number of seats despite losing support. Hindenburg disliked Hitler. A lot, in fact. Both times, he categorically refused to consider it.

However, between November 1932 and January 1933, the plotting of several politicians resulted in Hitler being named chancellor of Germany by Hindenburg. The chancellor in November, Kurt von Schleicher, had developed an economic plan to alleviate the pains of the Depression, but he could not find enough political support to make it a reality. He had gone to Hitler, but Hitler refused to throw in with Schleicher. When Schleicher had come to power, Schleicher had approached the left-wing of the Nazi Party behind Hitler's back. Worse still for Schleicher, he had essentially pushed the former chancellor, Franz von Papen, out of office in a sort of non-violent coup. That drove Hitler and von Papen into each other's political arms.

It was clear to everyone that Schleicher's plan was as unpopular as the man himself (it should be noted that his plan actually might have helped). Between November and January, von Papen and Hitler negotiated in fits and starts over a power-sharing agreement. In January 1933, the Reichstag took a month-long recess. Schleicher was a very unpopular man and had made many political enemies over the course of his career, especially during his short time as chancellor. Schleicher knew that when the Reichstag reconvened, there would be a no-confidence vote against him, so he went to Hindenburg, who, as president, had the power to name a chancellor or call elections. Hindenburg refused, and Schleicher had no choice but to resign.

That was when Hindenburg was approached by von Papen, who told Hindenburg, who by this time was clearly showing signs of senility, that he had worked out a power-sharing agreement with Hitler that allowed von Papen to both rein in Hitler and his party and stabilize political life in Germany. This time, reluctantly, Hindenburg agreed. Hitler became the chancellor of Germany on January 30th, 1933.

The former chancellor, Schleicher, for a number of reasons, was gunned down by a Nazi assassin on the Night of the Long Knives in June 1934.

Illustration 31: "The Field Marshal and the Corporal struggle with us for freedom and equality." Despite mutual enmity, the relationship between the two men was portrayed as friendly to the public.

Chapter 9 – The Nazis in Power

When Hitler came to power in 1933, he immediately set the state on two courses, with a third, the main one, yet to come. He was aided in his first two efforts by the fact that in the years from 1929 to 1932, Germany, under the last three chancellors and President Hindenburg, had moved decidedly to the right. They had increased the power of the federal government over the various *Länder* (states) and had used constitutional tricks to increase the office of chancellor.

They had also used the threat of street violence to get their way, but not in a way that seems obvious. With many Germans tired of the fighting between political parties, the chancellors promised that if they were given increased power, they would rein in organizations like the SA and the *Rotfront* ("Red Front"). They did this for a time, but they were not above using Hitler's men or the thought of them to intimidate opponents.

Secondly, they had slowly begun a patchwork program that was to undermine the power of the Reichstag. Many of these conservatives were monarchists, and another large group was hoping for a military dictatorship under Hindenburg, but he consistently refused. He was no friend of democracy, but he had taken an oath to uphold the Weimar Constitution, and a German officer's oath was everything.

When Hitler took power, he was somewhat limited in what he could do, "somewhat" being the keyword here. Under the power-sharing agreement he had made to become chancellor, the Nazis were only to hold three cabinet positions. Two were of relatively minor consequence. The third was the Ministry of the Interior, which gave Hitler power over the police.

The first thing Hitler did with his power as chancellor, along with the conservative, communist-hating members of his cabinet, was to go after the communists. Violence against the communists was already on the rise from the moment Hitler was sworn in, but about a month later, on February 28th, 1933, he was helped in that course by the actions of one man.

That man was Marinus van der Lubbe, a Dutch communist who was likely either emotionally disturbed or mentally challenged or both. For years, many historians, journalists, and the general public believed that the Nazis carried out the arson of the Reichstag, but in more recent times, more evidence has come to light showing that van der Lubbe carried out his plan without the Nazis' knowledge. Whether he acted at the urging of fellow communists in Germany or the Comintern (the international organization of communists run from and commanded by Moscow) is still being debated.

The Reichstag fire was a gift to Hitler and the Nazis. They were already bumping up against some opposition within the government, which was going to make implementing their program more difficult. The Reichstag fire provided the Nazis and all anti-communists (most importantly, the military and the police) with an excuse to crack down on communism in Germany. As a result, the Nazis, with the support of the conservative parties that still existed, declared a state of emergency, loudly declaring that "the country was under assault from communism." The Nazis, due to their widespread conservative support, suspended all civil liberties in

Germany for an unspecified amount of time. On March 23rd, 1933, the Reichstag, with Hindenburg's approval, passed the Enabling Act, which allowed Hitler to rule by decree for the next four years. And with that, freedom in Germany was dead.

Immediately, the Communist Party was outlawed. Soon after that, the Social Democratic Party, Germany's oldest political party, was outlawed as well. In each case, Hitler set the SA, the police, and his secret police on his enemies. (Germany had always had a secret police, but their powers had been somewhat limited in scope. That was no longer the case.)

The secret police, known to history as the "Gestapo," an amalgamating acronym of the German "GEheime STAatsPOlizei" (the acronym is capitalized only for illustration), was run and founded by Hermann Göring, the WWI *Luftwaffe* ace and early ally of Hitler. In 1934, Göring became the Minister of the Interior for the State of Prussia, as well as chief of the German Air Force (the *Luftwaffe*). Taking over the Gestapo in 1934 was Heinrich Himmler, the head of the SS.

With the Enabling Act, tens of thousands of Nazi opponents, both real and imagined, were rounded up and put in the concentration camps that were sprouting up all over Germany (some of them were actually built by the inmates, who were forced to sleep in the elements until construction was finished). The first major camp was at Dachau, just outside Munich, in Bavaria. This camp was run by Theodor Eicke, a sadist who laid the foundations for life in the camps. The guards of the camps were members of the SS, specifically the Death's Head Formations or *Totenkopfverbände*, which would later expand to include hundreds of thousands of men and an SS infantry division.

On May 1st, 1933, Germany celebrated May Day, which was recognized around the world for some time as the "Day of the Workers." The next day, Hitler outlawed all labor unions except the Nazis' own *Arbeitsfront* ("Work Front" or "Labor Front").

Thousands of the leading men and women of unions around the country were rounded up and thrown into the camps.

For the most part, most of the low-level communists and labor union members were released after some months in the camps. Their time spent there included hard labor, beatings, a starvation diet, and other torture. They were released on two conditions: they take an oath never to oppose Hitler or the Nazi Party (specifically meaning they could not join any secret reorganization of a union or party, but "opposition" could mean anything, including mouthing off to a policeman at the wrong time and place), and they never speak of the camps to anyone. On returning home with missing teeth, unset broken bones, and undernourishment, no one needed to talk of the camps, for it was obvious what went on there (though people, including camp staff, did talk, albeit in whispers).

Throughout Germany, the Nazis began what Hitler called *Gleichschaltung* or "coordination." This meant the "coordination" of German public life with the goals of the Nazi Party. This included implementing the Four-Year Plan to revitalize German economic life and bringing production under government supervision, "reforming" the courts and the legal system, and increasing the control and censorship of the press and all media under the Propaganda Ministry. The Nazis also changed the German education system to reflect Nazi beliefs and organized local committees to instruct the people on the proper way to behave (listening to the "proper" music, reading the "right" books, etc.) and to report on those that did not.

The most infamous symbol of the Nazis' efforts to reshape Germany in their image is the book burnings, which began in Berlin on May 10th, 1933, and spread around the country over the next few days. Libraries and bookstores were emptied of their proscribed ("forbidden") books and burned at the Berlin Opernplatz, a popular gathering spot and square. Books by some of Germany's leading authors of both past and present were burned, as well as foreign books, including books by Jack London (who was extremely popular in Germany but portrayed freedom-loving and anti-social characters), Helen Keller (as a deaf, mute, and blind person, she was considered "inferior" by the Nazis), and others.

Another author whose books were burned was famed German poet Heinrich Heine, whose political opinions and poems about freedom the Nazis found objectionable. Heine wrote in one of his books about the Christian crusades, "That was but a prelude: where they burn books, they will ultimately burn people as well." Today, Heine's quote is engraved at the memorial to the victims of Nazism at the spot of the Berlin book burning, which was led and encouraged by Josef Goebbels, the German propaganda minister.

Illustration 32: Book burning at the Opernplatz, May 10th, 1933.

Within about six months, the Nazis had "coordinated" most aspects of German public life. However, two groups remained in Hitler's crosshairs: the SA and the Jewish population of Germany.

As the Nazi Party grew, the SA and its head, Ernst Röhm, began to have dreams of their own. Among their aspirations were to be let loose to "deal" with the enemies of the Nazi Party and their own foes, specifically the Communist *Rotfront*. With the Reichstag fire and the Enabling Act, the SA was indeed set loose on those groups and many more. That left the SA with its main goal of supplanting the German Army itself.

There were several problems with this. Primarily, the army did not want to be supplanted, and it was the strongest armed force in the country. What's more, Hitler might need them to keep order or, more likely, to implement the military plans he laid out in *Mein Kampf*: the invasion and conquest of Eastern Europe and Russia.

Hitler could not afford to alienate the army in 1933. At this point in time, the army was still powerful enough to overthrow him should it decide to do so. So far, Hitler's actions had jibed with the army's interests, and while many in the army, especially at the top levels, were disgusted by the crude propaganda and street violence of the Nazis and the SA, they looked the other way as the Communist Party and the SPD were attacked and outlawed.

However, not only did they not approve of the men of the SA, whom they saw as crude, ill-disciplined thugs, which they were, they were also increasingly nervous about Röhm's and other SA leaders' calls for both supplanting the army and its political stance, which was more leftist than that of Hitler. For example, Hitler called for "coordination" between big business and the government. Röhm espoused ideas about the government takeover of big business.

The army also saw itself, and had for many years, as the most stable pillar of German society, and it was looked upon that way by most Germans. Army leaders also believed that they could act, either overtly or covertly, to limit Hitler's actions if it became necessary.

In the spring of 1934, the rhetoric of the SA leaders was getting more strident. They wanted to be more than just Hitler's "enforcers." They wanted a place of respect in the new Germany. Everyone knew that meant as the army, even if the SA did not come out and say it. All this reached Hitler's ears via informers within the

SA, some of whom acted on their own and some of whom were in the SS.

The SS was, at least in name, part of the SA, and its commander, Heinrich Himmler, was subordinate to Röhm. Himmler had risen to command the SS in 1929, taking the title *Reichsführer-SS*. The SS had begun as Hitler's bodyguard unit and was also used in the dissemination of party propaganda, but by the time of the Reichstag fire, Himmler had both increased membership (about sixty thousand men in 1933) and maneuvered his way into the overall command of the German police. The *Sicherheitsdienst*, also known as the SD or "Security Office," was part of the SS, and it was tasked with monitoring the party and other organizations for disloyalty. The Gestapo also fell under SD control.

While the SA was made up mainly of WWI combat veterans, street thugs, and men from the working classes, a significant portion of the SS was made up of college graduates, intellectuals, and former army and police officers. The SS was viewed, both within and without the Nazi Party, as being more disciplined and trustworthy than the SA.

Things with the SA came to a head at the end of June 1934. By this time, Hitler had heard enough rumors about Röhm's aspirations (including perhaps the replacement of Hitler) to be concerned with a "second revolution" led by the SA. On June 30th, he acted. Röhm and the SA party leadership were on holiday at a lakefront resort in northern Bavaria. Elements of the SS led by Himmler, along with the SD (led by Himmler's soon-to-be notorious right-hand man, Reinhard Heydrich) and Hermann Göring's personal police echelon, converged on the resort and arrested Röhm and the SA leadership. Making things worse for Röhm and many of the others was the fact that they were caught in bed with other men. This event, known to history as the Night of the Long Knives, resulted in Röhm's death—he committed suicide in his jail cell—and the deaths of eighty-five other SA leaders. This was the official death toll. The unofficial death toll likely approached one thousand as Himmler, Heydrich, and Göring, as well as their commanders, took the opportunity to strike at their own political and personal opponents.

Germany was shocked, but, in a way, it was also relieved. The SA had been an unpredictable and violent force on Germany's streets for a decade. Citizens were shocked that Hitler would act against one of his oldest allies, but in a speech shortly afterward, the Führer explained that his "love for Germany" and "law and order" compelled him to act, despite his personal history with those in the SA.

Most importantly, the army was relieved. Its place in Germany was secure. However, it had sold its soul to Hitler. In return for acting against the SA, Hitler demanded that every man, from private to field marshal, take a public oath of loyalty to him, personally, which they did. As was mentioned earlier when discussing Hindenburg's role as president, German officers and the army in general considered an oath absolutely binding, and Hitler was well aware of this. By the summer of 1934, Germany was Hitler's, especially after the death of Hindenburg in July, which allowed Hitler to combine the office of chancellor with that of the president.

Illustration 33: Himmler, Hitler, and Röhm.

The SA continued to exist, but it had been brought to heel by the Night of the Long Knives; from then on, it was used more for Nazi Party activities and the spread of propaganda rather than street violence. After decapitating the SA and bringing the army under his control, Hitler was free to engage in his two primary aims: bring the German armed forces back to full strength and remove the Jews from Germany.

To do the first and to solidify his position among the people, Hitler needed to make good on the main promise he had made throughout his campaigning years: restore the German economy. He would not be able to do anything without Germans working and producing again, and, of course, his popular support would wane if he didn't deliver.

For years after the end of WWII, many historians believed the Nazi propaganda about the revival of the German economy. Josef Goebbels, if he was alive today, would tell you that all propaganda contains a kernel of truth, no matter how small, and the truth is that Hitler did indeed revitalize certain elements of the German economy.

Since about the middle 1980s and especially after the fall of East Germany (which allowed scholars to view its many records that had previously been unobtainable), historians generally have revised their opinion of Hitler's "economic miracle." Those who were helped the most were those at the top and in the industries he needed in order to proceed with his main goals of re-militarization and military conquest. With the unions under control, the industrialists, who were the recipients of massive spending contracts, were firmly in Hitler's pocket. Some specialized workers, such as chemists and engineers, saw their incomes rise significantly under Hitler, but the bulk of German workers did not.

The industrial workers of Germany, the men who Hitler had made so many promises, got no significant increases in pay and now had no union protections. Though you will see documentaries detailing Hitler's recreation programs for the workers (known as the "Strength through Joy" program), with its cruises, day trips, and picnics, this was more for show. The bulk of the workers never went on any kind of joy cruise. And complaining did no good. Those who complained often ended up with a beating, a trip to the camps, or both. By this time, the Nazis had informants in virtually every large workplace in Germany.

The one statistic that everyone could point to was unemployment. Without a doubt, Hitler put the Germans back to work. Much of this was done through large public works projects, most prominently, the Autobahn highway system.

The Autobahn's purpose was to make it easier for Germany's coming mechanized army to move throughout the country, but it was labeled as "a road to the future." Hitler promised that most of the Germans would soon own cars and be able to take vacations throughout the country with ease, thanks to the Autobahn. If you ever travel to Germany on the original miles of the Autobahn, you will be amazed—the roads still go through some of the most beautiful countrysides in Europe. Hitler himself planned much of it with his artist's eye; in some cases, he had roads redirected and rest stops and vista points built so that the people traveling could enjoy some particularly gorgeous views, especially in the south of the country. However, most Germans didn't own cars and wouldn't own them throughout the Nazi period.

Still, unemployment was reduced by over two million in the first year and a half of the Hitler regime, and that alone gained the Führer increased support among many in the working, lower, and middle classes. Additionally, these numbers included women, who, despite the Nazi belief that women should remain at home and have children, entered the workforce in larger numbers as the Nazi years went on. There were 4.2 million women in the workforce in 1933 and 5.2 million in 1939. This number would increase again in the middle of the war when the Nazis realized they had better let women work in the factories.

How was Hitler's program financed, though? It was done through deficit spending, which was something many of the governments of the West did when they began to turn the corner on the Depression. The Germans were concerned that this deficit spending might mean a return to hyperinflation, which had scarred Germany so deeply. This was avoided by creating a phantom corporation called the Metallurgical Research Corporation or "Mefo" (its German acronym), which issued bonds and credits alongside currency. When the bond was due, it could be collected in regular currency.

In 1936, Hitler ordered the formation of a Four-Year Plan, which was how long he expected it would take for Germany to be ready for war. The aim of the Four-Year Plan was to increase Germany's exports while reducing its imports (imports largely meant raw materials and food). However, both because of the economic reality and Hitler's increasing unpopularity in the world, the Four-Year Plan never came close to its goals. By that point, no one really paid any attention, though, as WWII had begun in 1939, one year sooner than Hitler originally planned.

The increases in credits to large industries were all part of one goal. And this goal was not the betterment of life for the average German citizen but rather for re-militarization and war.

Throughout the late 1920s and into the 1930s, small numbers of men had been training to fly in Russia alongside the thousands of Germans who subverted the restrictions on flying lessons by flying gliders. As was mentioned in a previous chapter, this plan was concocted at the highest levels of the German General Staff. In addition to work being done in Russia, which included developing ideas for new fighter planes, the German Navy, which had been forbidden submarines, was working in Finnish waters with Finnish submarines in the hopes of having a German submarine fleet sometime in the near future. Politics and international relations make strange bedfellows, for Finland and the Soviet Union were enemies. The Finns wanted strong ties with Germany, which had aided them in their war of independence against Tsarist Russia during WWI, in case of a clash with the Soviet Union. For the Soviets' part, they received hard Western currency in exchange for letting the Germans use bases in Russia and Ukraine, even though Germany was known for its anti-communist rhetoric, both before and after Hitler's rise.

In 1933, Hitler had canceled all required reparations payments due under the Treaty of Versailles. Simply put, by this point in time, the nations of the West (meaning primarily Great Britain, France, and the United States) were in the midst of the Great Depression themselves and had turned inward. Additionally, in both English-speaking countries but especially in the UK, the feeling had arisen that the reparations imposed on Germany were both unfair and contributed to the Depression itself. Without the support of the English, the French were not willing to confront Hitler. Germany also withdrew from the League of Nations at this time.

In March 1935, Hitler announced that Germany was no longer going to abide by the military restrictions imposed by the Versailles Treaty, and he reintroduced conscription and the rearming of Germany. These moves alone, combined with the refusal to pay reparations, further increased Hitler's popularity in Germany. From 1935 onward, an ever-increasing percentage of the German national budget went toward rearmament, and an ever-increasing number of German workers were involved in it in some way to the point that Germany could point to near zero unemployment by 1938. However, this statistic disregards the fact that the "chronically unemployed" or *arbeitsscheu* ("work-shy") were forced into jobs for which they were not qualified or sent to the camps.

Illustration 34: Prisoners being driven into Dachau, a drawing by Michal Porulski, a Polish priest who was interned there during the war.

The War against the Jews Begins

Even before Hitler took power, the SA made life for Germany's Jews miserable. Most people, both Jewish and Gentile opponents of Nazism, knew what areas of the big cities were heavily populated by Nazis and tried to avoid them if possible. Germany's Jewish population, in contrast to other European nations (especially in the east), was highly assimilated and did not particularly stand out. However, those Jews who were Orthodox did, with their black clothing, hats, and hairstyles that gave them away. This was particularly the case for men, who knew that being caught alone in certain areas was asking for a beating.

You must remember that Germany before and after WWI was a highly regulated state; every family was required to register their address with the police. Jews and other minority groups (for example, Poles) often lived in certain neighborhoods, which was (and still is) something minorities and immigrants did in other countries, including the United States. Blond-haired German Jews might be identified simply by giving someone their street address. Before the Nazis, this was done when conversing with others or conducting business. After the Nazis came to power, this information was kept close to the vest.

When Hitler became chancellor, the SA went on an orgy of violence against the Jews, especially in the bigger cities and especially in Berlin. At the time, this shocked much of Germany, even those who were "mildly" anti-Semitic, as street violence and coarse behavior were considered "un-German." Many conservative allies of the Nazis were put off by the violence, and at the beginning, Hitler put a stop to much of it, knowing he had to solidify his power before taking any radical steps. The Nazis were even deterred, for a time, when they established a boycott of Jewish businesses. The international response forced Hitler to relent, but as his position got stronger within Germany, he was less and less responsive to pressure, both internally and externally.

By 1935, Hitler's hold on power was virtually complete, and with that, he ordered functionaries within the Nazi Party to draft what became known as the Nuremberg Laws. Every year in September, the Nazis would hold a rally in the southern city of Nuremberg, about one hundred miles north of Munich. In 1935, Hitler decided that the party rally would be a good time to announce his intention of formulating new laws governing race and the "Jewish question" in Germany. This initial set of laws was passed against the Jews, but soon after, other minorities, including the Roma (once derogatorily known as "Gypsies") and the small number of black people in the country, were targeted as well.

The Nuremberg Laws were actually two documents: The Law for the Protection of German Blood and German Honor and the Reich Citizenship Law.

The Law for the Protection of German Blood and Honor read as follows:

SECTION 1

1. Marriages between Jews and nationals of German or kindred blood are forbidden. Marriages concluded in defiance of this law are void, even if, for the purpose of evading this law, they are concluded abroad.

2. Proceedings for annulment may be initiated only by the Public Prosecutor.

SECTION 2

Relation outside marriage between Jews and nationals for German or kindred blood are forbidden.

SECTION 3

Jews will not be permitted to employ female nationals of German or kindred blood in their households.

SECTION 4

1. Jews are forbidden to hoist the Reich and national flag and to present the colors of the Reich.

2. On the other hand they are permitted to present the Jewish colors. The exercise of this authority is protected by the State.

SECTION 5

1. A person who acts contrary to the prohibition of section 1 will be punished with hard labor.

2. A person who acts contrary to the prohibition of section 2 will be punished with imprisonment or with hard labor.

3. A person who acts contrary to the provisions of section 3 or 4 will be punished with imprisonment up to a year and with a fine or with one of these penalties.

SECTION 6

The Reich Minister of the Interior in agreement with the Deputy of the Fuehrer will issue the legal and administrative regulations which are required for the implementation and supplementation of this law.

SECTION 7

The law will become effective on the day after the promulgation, section 3, however, only on 1 January 1936.

The Reich Citizenship Law read:

The Reichstag has unanimously enacted the following law, which is promulgated herewith:

Article 1

1. A subject of the state is a person who enjoys the protection of the German Reich and who in consequence has specific obligations toward it.

2. The status of subject of the state is acquired in accordance with the provisions of the Reich and the Reich Citizenship Law.

Article 2

1. A Reich citizen is a subject of the state who is of German or related blood, and proves by his conduct that he is willing and fit to faithfully serve the German people and Reich.

2. Reich citizenship is acquired through the granting of a Reich citizenship certificate.

3. The Reich citizen is the sole bearer of full political rights in accordance with the law.

Article 3

The Reich Minister of the Interior, in co-ordination with the Deputy of the Führer, will issue the legal and administrative orders required to implement and complete this law.

When these laws were published, whether in newspapers, magazines, or posters, they were frequently accompanied by the chart below to illustrate what constituted a "German," a *Mischling* (a person of mixed German-Jewish heritage), and a "Jew."

Illustration 35: The Nuremberg Laws illustrated. Original Nazi chart showing ancestry of (from l to r) Germans, "Mischlings 2nd Grade", "Mischlings 1st Grade" and Jewish people

Addenda to these laws forbade Jewish doctors from treating Germans, Jews from serving in the armed forces, or Jewish lawyers defending Germans; these examples are just the tip of the iceberg. However, exceptions could be made by Hitler himself. For instance, there was *Luftwaffe* General Helmuth Wilberg and *Luftwaffe* Field Marshal Erhard Milch, who had a bizarre family tree made up at the insistence of Göring.

With the passage of the Nuremberg Laws, street violence against Jews and the increased incarceration of Jews supposedly breaking the laws increased. Germans who were found having relations with Jews were publicly shamed, and those married to Jewish Germans were "encouraged" to divorce them (most did not).

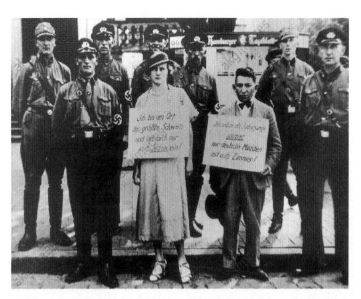

Illustration 35: Infamous picture of SA men with a German woman and Jewish man caught together. Her sign reads, "I am the biggest pig in the neighborhood and only lay with Jews." His sign reads, "I am a Jewish boy and only take German girls to my room." In German, their insults rhyme.

In about three years, Hitler had gone from losing votes in the last free German election to gaining absolute power over Germany. He had decreased unemployment and repudiated the Treaty of Versailles. In March 1936, he had ordered German troops into the demilitarized Rhineland against the terms of the treaty and gotten away with it, and he was even rebuilding the German armed forces. The capstone to all of this was the Berlin Olympics of 1936.

During the Olympic Games, the SA and other branches of the government and party, as well as the citizens, were overtly instructed and covertly told to "ease off" on the persecution of Jews. The most famous examples were the removal of signs in parks and on park benches that said "No Jews! Germans only!" German Jews interviewed during this time said they were afraid that once the world had left, having been fooled that the situation wasn't that bad in Germany, things would be worse for them. They were right to be fearful.

One more thing about the Berlin Olympics. In the United States, a big deal was made (and still is) over the fact that Jesse Owens, an African American, was the star of the games. It's no secret that this angered Hitler, but generally speaking, both the Führer and the German people considered the games a German victory. After all, Germany won the most gold medals at the games by far. However, not many people in the US were and are aware of this fact.

When the Olympics were over, things didn't return to "normal" for the Jews of Germany. They got worse. And making things far, far worse for not only the Jewish population of Germany but also Europe and the world were two international crises: the annexation of Austria to Germany in March 1938 and the Sudeten (or Czech) crisis in September. Both events were victories for Hitler. His popularity soared, and he saw that the British and French were incredibly reluctant to chance another war. By November 1938, Hitler felt unassailable.

On November 9th, 1938, Hitler ordered a new round of persecution of the Jewish population. The "excuse" for the order was the assassination of German diplomat Ernst vom Rath in Paris, who was killed by a young Polish Jew named Herschel Grynszpan. Grynszpan was angry about the prospect of being deported back to Germany and his family's inability to flee that country. Sadly, vom Rath was not an anti-Semite, and he was already under investigation by the Gestapo at the time of his death.

Hitler ordered the persecution that followed for revenge, and he apparently "encouraged" the Jews to leave the country. However, by that time, the laws on emigration and the money it cost to leave Germany made it virtually impossible for any but the wealthiest or most famous Jewish people to flee.

This persecution is infamously known to history as The Night of Broken Glass or *Kristallnacht* in German. Throughout Germany and Austria, Jewish businesses, synagogues, and homes were ransacked, with their windows smashed in (hence the name); oftentimes, these buildings were set alight. The fire departments were ordered to stand down. All across the country, those Jews brave enough to take to the streets in an attempt to save their businesses or places of worship were beaten, and they were often taken to camps or prisons. Even those who tried to remain out of sight in their homes were oftentimes dragged out into the street, beaten, mocked, and forced to do the most menial of tasks. In Vienna, crowds of Austrian Jews were forced to clean the streets for hours on their knees with toothbrushes while crowds gathered to jeer and spit on them.

Thousands of buildings were either totally or partially destroyed. Many of the synagogues of Germany and Austria, which had been standing for centuries, were gutted by fire, their holy books and much else tossed into the gutter. In the 1990s, former Hitler Youth member Alfons Heck appeared in a documentary about that group and growing up in Nazi Germany. He stated that it was his belief that "after Kristallnacht, none of us could pretend not to know what was going to happen to Germany's Jews." Everything was out in the open, and Hitler saw that the vast majority of Germans would not lift a finger to help their Jewish neighbors. They were either indifferent, anti-Semitic, or afraid of what might happen to them if they interfered. It is the assertion of many historians that *Kristallnacht* did indeed encourage Hitler, Himmler, and the Nazis to go further in their plan to "rid" Germany of its Jews.

Illustration 36: The Night of Broken Glass, November 9ᵗʰ, 1938.

International Affairs

When he heard the muted international response to his repudiation of the Versailles Treaty and rearmament, Hitler realized that Britain and France were both afraid of another European war and were too focused on the effects of the Depression within their own countries to interfere with his plans in any significant way.

When Hitler ordered his troops into the Rhineland on March 7ᵗʰ, 1936, he told his troops to return across the Rhine should the French open fire on them. He knew that his country was not ready to fight a war, at least not yet. When the French did not open fire, instead choosing to bring their troops home, Hitler sensed he could get away with more.

In March 1938, after years of agitation by Austrian Nazis (including the assassination of Austrian chancellor Engelbert Dollfuss in 1934), riots and anti-government actions were launched throughout the country, especially in the capital of Vienna. They were close to launching a long-planned coup d'état when the Austrian chancellor, Kurt von Schuschnigg, offered, albeit under pressure, to install a number of Nazis in his cabinet. A few months later, Schuschnigg called a special election for the Austrian people to vote on the question that Hitler had been screaming about for years: the union of Germany and Austria.

On March 11th, days before the election was to be held, Hitler sent an ultimatum to the Austrian chancellor, threatening a full-scale invasion and mass destruction should he not resign and name an Austrian Nazi as his successor. After much maneuvering, miscommunication, further threats, and an order to begin the invasion on March 12th, Schuschnigg resigned. On the morning of March 12th, the new Austrian chancellor, Arthur Seyss-Inquart, who was later hanged for crimes against humanity for his role in the Holocaust in Holland, "invited" Hitler across the border.

When Hitler crossed the border and entered Vienna, he was given a hero's welcome. Many Austrians supported the move, as it restored them to a powerful position, one they had not held since before the fall of the Habsburg Empire in 1918. It also brought order after years of infighting. The Nazi takeover of Austria, which became known as the state of Ostmark under Hitler, also brought out the worst in many Austrians, especially in the capital, where Hitler had first been exposed to anti-Semitism. Though it might seem strange to hear today, many German Nazis were shocked at the level of viciousness toward the Jewish population that took place in Austria. Remember, though, this was before the extermination of the Jews had begun, so many Nazis were not completely inured to the violence directed against the Jews.

Though the Treaty of Versailles had expressly forbidden the union of Germany and Austria, the British and French sat on the sidelines, as did the leader of the Soviet Union, Joseph Stalin, who was eager for the powers of Europe to fight each other. Excuses were made in the British Parliament and the French National Assembly, as well as in the press of both countries. "It's a German affair." "The Austrians wanted it." "Do you want to fight another bloody war over Austria?"

One voice stood out above the crowd, however. This voice was a member of Parliament, and he had been the First Lord of the Admiralty during WWI. This man was Winston Churchill, and he decried and attempted to shame his government's inaction in response to Hitler's aggression but to no avail.

Throughout Hitler's book *Mein Kampf,* as well as hundreds, if not thousands of times in his speeches, he had proclaimed his desire to bring together all the Germans of Europe into one nation. Throughout history, groups of Germans had moved to other parts of Europe in search of a better life or had been on the "wrong" side of border changes following a war, such as WWI.

Illustration 37: Ethnic German populations, c. 1910. There was also a sizable number of Germans in the Volga Basin in Russia. (Courtesy Rex Germanus, Wikicommons).

As you can see on the map above, the area that today is the Czech Republic (in 1938, it was Czechoslovakia) bulges into the area between Germany and Austria. In the border areas between the three countries but within Czechoslovakia were the Sudeten Germans, who took their name from a local river. Soon after the annexation of Austria, Hitler began demanding that the

Sudetenland be incorporated into Germany. He accused the Czech government of encouraging anti-German laws and persecution and ignoring the plight of the German minority within their country.

The truth is that there were some laws, especially regarding language, that were anti-German, and some anti-German incidents did occur. However, these were blown out of proportion by the Nazis in their propaganda, and they completely ignored the Sudeten Nazis' acts of violence against the Czechs in German-majority areas.

The Czechs categorically refused Hitler's demands, and they could have held out for some time against Hitler's armies if they had been given guarantees from France, Britain, and the USSR that they would come to the Czechs' aid. The Czechoslovak Army was strong and had strong border defenses in defensible terrain. The Skoda Works produced some of the best cannons and tanks in the world. Ultimately, however, the Czechs would not be able to defeat Hitler without help.

Stalin announced that he would come to the aid of the Czechoslovakians if the British and French did. But they did not. Eager to avoid another European war, Prime Minister Neville Chamberlain and his French counterpart, Édouard Daladier, took several trips to Munich to meet with Hitler and his new ally, Benito Mussolini of Italy, to see if there was a way to appease the German dictator and avoid war. And, of course, there was: give Hitler the Sudetenland. So, that is what they did—and not one Czechoslovakian official was invited to the talks that would decide the fate of their nation. Without the mountains and forests of the Sudetenland, Czechoslovakia was indefensible.

Abandoned by its "friends," the Czechs agreed to Hitler's terms and evacuated the Sudetenland. Hitler had won again, without firing a shot. In England, Neville Chamberlain got off his plane and waved his agreement with Hitler in the air. "I believe this is peace in our time," he said. In Parliament, a short time afterward, Chamberlain was given a rousing round of applause for keeping the peace, but

Churchill, now with a larger number of followers, stood up and said, in part, "You were given the choice between war and dishonour. You chose dishonour, and you will have war." One year later, Hitler marched his troops into the rest of Czechoslovakia unopposed.

Shortly after Chamberlain and Daladier left Munich, Hitler commented to those around him, "We have met our enemies, and they are worms." Seeing how easily the British and French abandoned their "ally" in Czechoslovakia, Joseph Stalin was determined to come to terms, at least temporarily, with Hitler.

Illustration 38: The Munich Conference, September 1938. Left to right are Chamberlain, Daladier, Hitler, Mussolini, and Ciano (Mussolini's son-in-law and aide).

For two decades, Hitler had made it plain that he had three main goals: *Lebensraum* ("living space") in the USSR, the removal of the Jews from Germany, and the destruction of world communism, which he and other Nazis believed was being run by a Jewish cabal from Moscow.

Similarly, Russia had always been on the alert for Prussian or German power. For many years, the Prussians and Russians shared a long border in occupied Poland. Under the communists, and especially since the rise of Stalin, Hitler was seen as the archenemy, both of the Soviet Union as a nation and of communism as a political ideology.

However, after the disaster of the Munich Conference (at least for the Western Allies and the USSR), Stalin realized that he would be on his own as well if Hitler attacked the Soviet Union, especially since the USSR was their ideological enemy. Stalin knew that, for a variety of reasons (mostly of his own making), the Soviet Union would not be able to resist Hitler effectively in 1938. He would need to buy some time.

While Stalin was pondering his next move, Hitler was planning his: the conquest of Poland. He began his plan in the same way he had begun the operations against Austria and Czechoslovakia, with the need to bring all ethnic Germans into the Reich and under his protection. As you can see in Illustration 37, there were many ethnic Germans living in Poland. Many had lived there for centuries, along the ever-changing borders between empires and countries. Others had found themselves in Poland after the end of WWI when the Allied Powers carved out the Polish nation from what had been the Russian, Austrian, and German Empires. The biggest point of contention was the so-called "Polish Corridor," which separated much of East Prussia from Germany proper. It was as if much of Prussia, the home of German unification, was now an island surrounded by the Poles. Within the Polish Corridor was the Free City of Danzig (today's Gdansk, Poland), which was under the protection of the League of Nations and was neither Polish nor German, though, by 1936, most of the city's governing senate was made up of local Nazis.

Hitler and his propaganda minister, Josef Goebbels, stepped up the anti-Polish propaganda, which stated in a variety of ways that the Germans in Danzig and in the Polish borderlands were being mistreated. In Danzig, this was not the case, as the city had a German majority. In the Polish/German border area, there were some anti-German incidents, but these paled in comparison to the anti-Polish activities that went on in Germany after WWI. When Hitler came to power, many Poles, whose families had lived in Germany for decades or more, emigrated to Poland for their own safety.

Throughout the summer of 1939, Hitler became shriller in his demands for what he called a "settlement of the Polish question." This was simply a euphemism for his intended invasion of Poland, which virtually everyone on the planet knew was coming. Between the annexation of the Sudetenland and the summer of 1939, both France and especially Britain had begun massive rearmament programs to discourage Hitler from any further moves in Europe, but it was "too little, too late." They each gave the Poles a guarantee that they would declare war on Germany should Hitler invade their nation.

The Poles hoped that this guarantee would deter Hitler, but Stalin and many others realized that it was likely Hitler would "finish off" Poland before the British and French could do anything substantial. They could not directly come to the aid of Poland, and while mounting an invasion of western Germany was not likely, it would take time to prepare even if there was the will for it, which there was not.

Both Hitler and Stalin knew this, and both were worried about what the other would do. Hitler worried that the Russians might come to the aid of their fellow Slavs in Poland, while Stalin worried that a successful German invasion of Poland would put Hitler right on his border.

On August 23rd, 1939, the governments of Germany and the Soviet Union announced a nonaggression pact. They pledged not to attack one another for ten years, along with massive trade deals and a secret agreement that involved dividing Poland between them. To say the world was shocked, after all the violent rhetoric between the two nations over the years, would be putting it mildly.

WONDER HOW LONG THE HONEYMOON WILL LAST?

The Soviet Union and Germany were not only ideological enemies; they had also supported opposite sides in the brutal Spanish Civil War, which lasted from 1936 to 1939. Both sides sent tanks, pilots, planes, and arms to their allies in Spain (the Germans supported nationalist/fascist General Francisco Franco, while the Soviets supported the communists and socialists). The war in Spain gave the world a taste of what another world war would be like. In 1937, German planes destroyed the city of Guernica in northern Spain, killing perhaps one thousand civilians.

Illustration 39: Hitler: "Scum of the Earth, I presume?" Stalin: "Bloody assassin of the workers, I presume?"

On September 1st, 1939, Hitler ordered his troops into Poland. On September 3rd, France and Britain declared war on Germany—WWII in Europe had begun. On September 17th, the Red Army of the Soviet Union invaded and occupied the eastern portion of Poland per their agreement with Germany.

The invasion of Poland showcased the "new" German Army (the *Wehrmacht*) and its powerful *Luftwaffe*. Most stunning of all to people around the world was the Germans' use of tanks. Though tanks had been used in the latter days of WWI, the machines of that era, along with the thinking of its generals, were slow, ponderous, and unreliable. The German tanks of 1939 were neither.

Using armor and aircraft (mostly dive bombers and fighter planes) in close coordination, the Nazis would attack one specific point in the enemy's lines, usually where it was weak. The tanks would break through the lines and fan out to surround the enemy's neighboring positions and drive deeper into enemy territory to disrupt supplies and communications. They would be closely followed by infantry units, which initially advanced behind short but intense rolling artillery barrages (a rolling barrage is one that strikes just in front of the advancing infantry, with the idea being that the barrage will disrupt and disorient the enemy so he is not able to effectively fight back).

Though the Poles fought bravely against both foes, they were doomed. The fighting went on for six weeks, with the Poles finally surrendering when the *Luftwaffe* began reducing the Polish capital, Warsaw, to rubble. The Poles were the first to succumb to the Nazi military machine, and as a ratio of their pre-war population, no nation suffered more losses during WWII and the Holocaust than Poland. Just under *20 percent* of Poland's people (and *90 percent* of its Jewish population) died during the war. That's almost one out of every five people.

In response to the Nazi invasion of Poland, France launched an invasion of the German border state of the Saar, which was a province they had occupied at the end of WWI. This invasion, which was met with little resistance, penetrated about six miles and then stopped and went no farther. No adequate explanation has ever been given for the halt. After the war, Field Marshal Alfred Jodl, when he was on trial for crimes against humanity, stated that if the British and French, who had had a total of 110 divisions along the front in the west, had invaded, the Germans would not have been able to stop them, having only 23 divisions facing westward when they invaded Poland. Hitler had gambled and won.

In November of 1939, Stalin demanded that Finland give up some of its crucial naval and coastal installations in the southern Baltic Sea and its southern coast, with its sizable area of the Karelian Isthmus that connects Finland to Russia near Leningrad (today's St. Petersburg). His reasoning was that since Finland had been aided by the Germans in its war of independence against Russia during WWI and since Hitler needed to keep Scandinavia secure because of the natural resources there, Hitler might ally himself with Finland in any future moves against the USSR.

The interesting thing is that in the German-Soviet Nonaggression Pact, Hitler had given Stalin free rein to deal with Finland as he wished, as well as giving Stalin the go-ahead to re-annex the Baltic states of Lithuania, Latvia, and Estonia, which had belonged to Russia until 1918. That was the price Hitler was willing to pay to be able to attack Poland without worrying about the Soviet Union.

The Finns rejected Stalin's demands, and shortly thereafter, the Soviet Red Army attacked Finland, starting what is known as the Winter War. In England and France, there was talk of perhaps having to declare war against both the Soviet Union and Germany, as it seemed the two totalitarian powers were aligning. However, the Finns mounted a stubborn defense, which cost the Soviets nearly a million men killed, wounded, and missing.

In the end, however, Finland could not hope to hold out against the numbers of the Soviet Union, so the Finns came to terms with Stalin in the early spring of 1940. This had several effects on the course of the war. First, the ineptitude of the Soviets, at least during the first half of the short war against the Finns, convinced Hitler that the Red Army was a paper tiger and that it was poorly led, poorly trained, and badly equipped. The Finns' stand convinced Hitler that it was possible to defeat the Soviets.

Second, though the Western Allies by no means supported the USSR in its invasion of Finland, they did not need to concern themselves with questions about declaring war on the USSR as well as Hitler. The Winter War ended quickly, and by the time it ended, Hitler was already making threatening moves in the west.

And lastly, by the time the Finns gave in to Stalin's demands, there were small signs that the agreement between Germany and the USSR was beginning to fray, and over time, these signs would get bigger. Though it would be another year and some months before Hitler launched his invasion of the Soviet Union, the Allies were gathering information from its own intelligence agents within Germany and the USSR that things were not going swimmingly between the two dictatorships. This information was corroborated by informants within the German Army and government, as well as increasingly "undiplomatic" language coming from the German Ministry of Propaganda. As time went by, the Germans would begin to renege on much of their agreement, such as holding onto shipments that were supposed to go to the Soviets. The Soviets likewise reneged, sending raw materials westward, for example. However, this was a relatively slow process, and it would take until the spring of 1941 to hit its high point. By that time, Hitler had already ordered his invasion of the USSR to begin by the middle of May (it would be delayed for several reasons until late June).

All of that was in the future in 1939 and early 1940. On the Western Front, where nearly a million French soldiers sat in the fortifications of the Maginot Line (their incredibly expensive and highly technical defense line with Germany) along with the British Expeditionary Force (BEF), the soldiers took to calling the war the "Phony War." From September 1939 until May 1940, nothing of note happened on the Western Front.

In the early part of the war, Hitler was happy to have his general staff plan his campaigns. He would occasionally interfere or make suggestions, but, by and large, the campaigns against Poland, Western Europe, the Balkans, and the first part of the invasion of the Soviet Union were left to the generals. It was only after things began to turn for the Germans that Hitler got involved in the minutiae of the war, making things far worse for the German Army.

So, in 1939 and 1940, the German General Staff planned the campaigns under the general direction of Hitler. Many in the German Army were hesitant to attack France, but some of the younger, bolder, and more innovative generals believed it was possible to not only beat the French but also beat them swiftly.

From the early 1920s until almost the war began, the French had invested hundreds of millions of francs (an estimated seven to ten billion US dollars in 2021) in the most innovative and powerful line of defense ever seen. The Maginot Line ran along the Franco-German border, and many considered it impenetrable, including the Germans.

The problem for the French was Belgium. During WWI, the Germans had stormed through Belgium, violating its neutrality, to attack France. Throughout the 1920s, no appreciable work was done on fortifications on the Franco-Belgian border. Firstly, it was believed, or rather hoped, that Germany would remain a peaceful democratic power far into the future after having "learned its lesson." Secondly, it was hoped that should there be a threat of war from Germany again, Belgium would tie itself with the Allies after having experienced a harsh German occupation from 1914 to 1918. Building a strong defensive line of fortifications on France's border with Belgium would signal to the Belgians that the French had no intention of defending them and would instead stay behind the Maginot Line.

Throughout the 1920s and into the 1930s, the French and British assured the Belgians that should Germany attack again, they would immediately come to Belgium's aid as they had in WWI. However, after Hitler took power and especially after the British and French had abandoned Czechoslovakia, the Belgians began to waver and went back and forth in diplomatic circles, discussing whether they should declare neutrality once again and if Hitler would even respect it if they did.

Naturally, Hitler assured the Belgians as much as possible that he would respect their neutrality. However, the Belgians continued waffling, which only added to French insecurity. Thus, the French, belatedly, continued building the Maginot Line along the Franco-Belgian border. By the time of the German invasion, this addition consisted of a small number of forts that were widely spaced apart—the perfect position for an attacker.

While the Germans were planning their attack on France, developments in Scandinavia distracted both the Allies and Germany. Britain received word that Hitler intended to invade Norway, both to protect his northern flank and to protect the massive iron, nickel, and timber resources he received from Sweden. The British were also concerned that the Germans could use Norway's hundreds of fjords to hide their growing U-boat fleet, which was already beginning to take a serious toll on British shipping.

Hitler had thought of a Norwegian invasion, but he instead offered the Norwegians a nonaggression pact, part of which would allow German naval vessels to use Norwegian waters. This would be intolerable to the British, whose security lay at sea, so the British, along with a small number of French forces, launched a preemptive invasion of Norway. After receiving a negative reply to his overture from the Norwegians and having gotten word of British plans, Hitler launched an invasion of Denmark and Norway on April 9th, 1940.

The German assault on Norway happened on the same day the Allies landed at various strategic points in central and northern Norway. Though the battle lasted until June 10th, it was all but over by the middle of May, with the Germans, having sustained significant naval losses, successfully forcing the Allied troops to evacuate. (Denmark was overrun in a day, and it was used as a stepping stone for German troops to move to Norway and to assert German control over access to the Baltic Sea.)

The Norwegian campaign did not affect Hitler's plans to invade France in any significant way, except perhaps to raise the morale of the German armed forces and the German people while the Allies' morale took a significant hit.

On May 10th, 1940, Hitler ordered his generals forward. The German attack was launched all along Germany's western border. Holland, which had been neutral and unmolested in WWI, declared its neutrality again, but that did not save it. And the Dutch were no match for the Germans, who, along with the first airborne (paratrooper) attack in history, had also firebombed the major Dutch city of Rotterdam, reducing much of it to ashes. Five days after it had begun, the war in Holland was over.

To the south of Holland, the Germans invaded Belgium, just as everyone had expected. When they did, the BEF and much of the French Army moved into Belgium to meet the German attack, which was exactly what they had promised the Belgians and exactly what the Germans had hoped they would do.

To the south, along the Franco-German frontier, large numbers of German troops, cannons, and planes made a show of attacking in a number of places along the Maginot Line, holding the French in their tracks, just as the Germans had hoped.

In between the Franco-Belgian border and the start of the Maginot Line proper was the thick, hilly, and difficult-to-traverse Ardennes Forest. It was difficult to traverse since there were few roads, and the roads that existed were many times in poor condition or not very wide. "Surely," the French thought, "the Germans can't move tanks and large cannons through the Ardennes." Of course, you either know already from prior reading or can guess that was exactly what the Germans did, as you can see on the excellent map below.

*Illustration 36: The German moves north of the main part of the
Maginot Line (blue hash marks). Though this map is in
Vietnamese, it is an excellent and clear overview of the German
attack in the west. Once the Germans reached the English Channel,
they turned southward to attack or fend off French countermoves
coming from the area of the Maginot Line.*

The bulk of the German armored forces were in the Ardennes
spearhead. Once they cleared the forest, they made a rapid dash to
the English Channel, and once they were there, the main British
and French force in Belgium was trapped. French forces to the
south launched several counterattacks but, with only one real
exception, did not make any progress.

What's interesting about the German tank (*Panzer* in German)
spearhead is that, for the most part, German tanks were inferior to
their French counterparts. Since the end of the war, a legend about
the German tank forces of WWII has taken hold. What's odd
about this is that, generally speaking, the Germans Panzers were not
better than their opponents' tanks until late 1942 and early 1943
with the advent of the Panther, Tiger, and the up-gunned Panzer
IV.

What the Germans did have, almost throughout the war, was better tank commanders, and that was most clearly the case in the French campaign. Germany's most famous WWII general, Erwin Rommel, was one of those leading the spearhead into France. Another was Heinz Guderian, who had helped formulate German tank doctrine before the war began.

The Germans used their tanks as a relatively independent arm of their armed forces. Tanks would break through the front lines, with mobile infantry in support to deal with anti-tank infantry. The German attack, dubbed *Blitzkrieg* ("lightning war"), called for deep armored penetration of enemy lines and/or the envelopment of their front-line forces. The Germans used the tank as their main weapon of war, whereas the French and British used theirs as infantry support weapons, dispersing them throughout their forces and thereby weakening their effect.

The campaign was basically over before it began. The BEF, along with some French and Belgian troops, were surrounded at the French coastal town of Dunkirk, from which they were evacuated through a Herculean effort on the part of the British Royal Navy and Royal Air Force, along with French troops, helping to prevent a German breakthrough. The successful evacuation of over 350,000 troops may have saved Britain, whose prime minister was now Winston Churchill. Churchill had taken office on the very day the Germans invaded France, and although he was faced with the greatest military disaster in British history, he vowed to fight to the end.

On June 25th, 1940, the French officially surrendered to Hitler and Mussolini, whose troops belatedly attacked in southern France. This armistice was signed in the same train car that the WWI armistice had been signed in. The French were "lucky." To avoid the cost in money and manpower it would take to occupy all of France, Hitler allowed the French to run a semi-autonomous region in the south, which was run by a former French war hero turned fascist named Marshal Pétain. This regime was centered in the city of Vichy.

Hitler visited Paris only once. He took a speedy tour through the city, which was filmed and which you can easily find on the internet or TV, seeing the Eiffel Tower, Notre-Dame, and, what was the most important spot to him, Napoleon's tomb. He never visited France again.

In Germany, even people who had been quietly on the fence about Hitler now had to admit there was something to the man. He had taken Germany from being the pariah of Europe to its most powerful state and its master. Germans began to enjoy the fruits of conquest as well, as looted, seized, and surrendered goods of all kinds began making their way into Germany.

The amazing thing was that all of this happened just as Hitler had predicted, which was also the problem. Hitler was powerful before the war, but now his position was unassailable. He would not be removed except through assassination or defeat, neither of which seemed likely in 1940.

The other problem was this, though it did not seem to be a problem at the time: Germany's economy had not even gone over to a war footing. Defense had taken up a great part of the budget before the war, and it continued at almost the same level through 1940 and arguably until the start of 1942. Germans had enough of everything and had not been asked to sacrifice in any deep way, at least economically. Even the casualties of the Polish and French campaigns had not been high, especially when compared to the Great War. It seemed as if Hitler had pulled off a miracle.

Illustration 37: Hitler and Göring on the balcony of the Reich Chancellery after the defeat of France in 1940.

Yet, within all this success was the kernel of the seed of defeat. Hitler, along with his lieutenants, especially Hermann Göring, the head of the *Luftwaffe*, began to believe they were both infallible and invincible. They got their first taste of how wrong they were when Hitler attempted to bring Great Britain to heel.

From late July and increasing through August and into September, the *Luftwaffe* and Britain's outnumbered Royal Air Force battled for air supremacy over southern England and the English Channel. Hitler planned on conquering Britain or, at the very least, forcing her out of the war to have a secure rear flank when he attacked the Soviet Union, which was his life's goal at that point.

To do this, he needed to do several things. He had already launched the U-boats against British and merchant ships arriving and leaving the UK. This attempt to starve Britain into submission and prevent aid from the US would continue throughout the war, but it would reach its height in 1942. After the war, Churchill would say the only thing that truly frightened him throughout the war was the U-boat campaign. At one point in 1941, the British had only enough food for two weeks.

Hitler also needed to establish control over the English Channel, at least for a short time, in order to move his planned invasion force to the British Isles. The Royal Navy was too powerful for the German *Kriegsmarine* to take on, though Hitler, like Kaiser Wilhelm II before him, attempted to rival it, at least for a time. However, if the *Luftwaffe* could destroy the Royal Air Force, he could send his invasion force across the Channel with an unrivaled air escort to fend off British ships.

That meant he had to destroy the Royal Air Force, though. Hermann Göring assured Hitler that it would only take a matter of days, weeks at the most, and at first, it seemed like this might happen. The Germans concentrated on bombing British airbases and destroying hangars, runways, and aircraft on the ground.

Though the British brought down a higher number of planes in comparison to the Germans, the Germans could afford to lose them—the British could not. For a time, the British were able to repair the damage to their airfields and continue, but by the end of August and beginning of September, they were on their last legs and were not able to keep up with the destruction.

It was at this point that fate stepped in. In late August, a German bomber crew made a navigational error and dropped its bombs over London. Hitler had expressly forbidden attacks on British cities. He had an affinity for the British as fellow "Germanic" peoples, and he wished to use his hesitancy to bomb civilians as a bargaining chip if the British sought terms. However, the next night, Churchill, who had forbidden attacks on German cities as well, ordered a small number of bombers to Berlin as revenge. Neither raid did much damage, but both infuriated the other side. From that point forward, German planes began to concentrate on the destruction of British cities and the morale of their civilians.

Though "the Blitz," as the British called it, ultimately cost the UK forty thousand people (twenty thousand in London alone) from 1940 to 1941 (they lost seventy thousand throughout the whole war), the change in German tactics allowed the Royal Air Force to repair its airfields unmolested, build more planes, and mount a concentrated resistance to German attacks.

In this, they were helped by the advent of radar, a British invention that was totally overlooked by the Germans, though they shortly developed their own. Radar, combined with ships at sea, "coastwatchers" (civilians watching the air over coastal England), and intelligence sources and spies in Western Europe, helped the British anticipate German attacks.

This was also helped by an incredible fighting spirit. It was not unknown for two or three British fighters to attack German formations of twenty or more planes. Also aiding the British was the fact that they were flying over their homeland. They could attack a German formation flying over the coast, land and refuel, and then attack the same formation as they flew home. Naturally, this caused more damage to the Germans, and it also made them think the British had many more planes than they actually did. Additionally, British pilots who managed to bail out of damaged planes landed over friendly territory, sometimes even returning to base and flying again the very same day. Those shot down over the Channel, if they survived the impact, were often picked up by the Royal Navy. The Germans had a limited amount of fuel and could only spend minutes over their targets, and those who survived a dogfight and bailed out came down on British soil or were picked up by the British navy.

The Blitz went on until the spring of 1941 and continued again in 1944 with the advent of the V-1 and V-2 rockets, but by mid-September, the German effort had weakened. By the spring, most German aircraft were deployed eastward for the coming invasion of the USSR. Hitler dismissed his defeat over Britain as inconsequential. To him, the English were all but defeated, and he would deal with them in his own good time. Many of his more insightful officers were sure this was not the case. They knew the

English would not give up, and what's more, an unconquered England meant supplies (and perhaps even troops) from the United States would increase month by month.

But the Führer ordered them to prepare for a war against the Soviets, and orders were meant to be followed.

War in the East

Hitler launched his attack against the Soviet Union on June 22nd, 1941. He originally ordered his generals to be ready to launch the offensive on May 15th, but several factors caused a delay.

For many years, people believed that the delay was due to Hitler having to come to the aid of his ally Benito Mussolini in the latter's disastrous invasion of Greece. Though this did play a role in the delay, other issues contributed to it as well, the most important of which were a lack of oil and gasoline and the Germans needing more time to gather transport for the campaign.

This latter fact was dismissed for many years, partly due to the successful propaganda put out by the Nazis themselves. During the war and for years afterward, the image of the German Panzers thundering across Europe was what people thought of when they pictured the German Army in action, but in reality, most of the German Army moved by horse and wagon. This remained the case until the end of the war. Literally hundreds of thousands of horses and their fodder had to be gathered before the invasion of the Soviet Union, and this, combined with a lack of fuel and oil for their machines in the spring of 1941, which was only made worse by the invasions of Yugoslavia and Greece, delayed the Soviet operation until late June.

That delay came about because Mussolini was jealous of Germany's imperial gains. Mussolini fashioned himself as a modern-day Caesar and wished to establish a new Roman empire in southern Europe and North Africa.

In North Africa, Mussolini had launched an invasion of British-controlled Egypt and Kenya from his colonies in Libya and Somalia only to be humiliated by the smaller but better led British forces. Hitler had to come to his friend's rescue then as well, sending the Afrika Korps under Erwin Rommel to Africa, where he fought an intense campaign against the British and later the Americans until the spring of 1943.

In October 1940, Mussolini launched an invasion of Greece and was humiliated when the much smaller Grecian armed forces pushed him back into Albania, which was an Italian colony and Mussolini's starting point. Hitler, worried that the British would use Greece and the Balkans as a second front against him to penetrate his southern flank, sent a sizable number of divisions and planes southward.

At the start, he had gotten permission from the Yugoslavian regent Prince Paul to move his troops through that country, but at the last minute, pro-British forces overthrew the regent and replaced him with the fifteen-year-old Peter II. Peter and his advisors immediately refused Hitler passage. In response, Hitler launched Operation Punishment (also known as Operation Retribution) against the Yugoslavs.

Though Hitler successfully defeated the Yugoslav Army in the field and moved his troops on to Greece, the occupation of Yugoslavia was resisted fiercely throughout the war, forcing Hitler to keep between 250,000 to 300,000 troops in the country, which could have been of use to him elsewhere. The occupation of Yugoslavia was incredibly brutal, even by Nazi standards, and it also devolved into a civil war between rival Yugoslavian groups based on ideology, ethnicity, or both.

With the occupation of Yugoslavia done, Hitler moved into Greece on April 6th, 1941, which, by that time, had seen the arrival of sizable British and British Imperial troops. Despite a stubborn defense, the Greeks and British troops were no match for the

Germans, and by June, the Germans occupied the country, including the large island of Crete, which saw a major battle between British and Imperial forces (notably troops from New Zealand and Australia) and German paratroopers. This was the largest use of paratroopers at that point in the war, and the casualties suffered by the Germans caused Hitler to forbid the use of paratroopers for the rest of the conflict, though they did fight with incredible tenacity in Italy and France.

By June 22nd, Hitler was ready to invade the Soviet Union, despite his agreement with Stalin in 1939. Stalin received many warnings about Hitler's intentions, but he inexplicably chose to ignore them. Goods still streamed to Germany, even as German troops were moving to take their positions for the invasion, and literally hundreds of German planes had been seen behind Soviet lines scouting Red Army positions. Additionally, spies from all over the world had sent Stalin warnings of an impending invasion, and Winston Churchill himself, who was privy to information gleaned from one of the most successful code-breaking operations in history, warned Stalin an invasion was coming. In the latter case, Stalin chose to believe that Churchill, who was an anti-communist if there ever was one, was trying to bait him into attacking Germany. When the German invasion did come, Stalin at first refused to believe the reports he was getting from his own commanders. Stalin only believed it when the evidence became absolutely irrefutable, and when he did, he went into a depression that lasted weeks, which only helped the German cause.

The German invasion of the USSR involved almost four million men, over 3,500 tanks and assault vehicles, nearly 5,000 planes of all types, nearly 30,000 cannons and mortars of all sizes, more than half a million horses, and an equal number of trucks and other transport vehicles.

Facing the Germans on the Soviet western border were nearly three million men, more than ten thousand tanks, and an equal number of aircraft of all types. Unfortunately for the Soviets, a variety of factors hindered their defense. First and foremost, Stalin had killed many of the Red Army's top commanders in the purges of the late 1930s, believing them to be part of a conspiracy against him (they were not). This meant that that the top commanders in both the field and to the rear were hesitant to act on their own lest it result in their own deaths. In addition, many of those commanders had been junior officers during the purges and were not prepared for the responsibilities thrust upon them. So, when they did act, it was frequently the wrong thing to do.

Though a new training regimen had been put into place following the Winter War against the Finns, most Soviet troops were poorly trained, poorly led, and poorly equipped. Though in many cases they fought to the death, just as many or more were captured in the huge envelopment battles that took place when the Germans invaded. This situation would continue at different times and places throughout the first part of the German campaign, known as Operation Barbarossa.

Illustration 38: Operation Barbarossa through the fall of 1941.

Hitler and several of his generals believed they could employ the same blitzkrieg tactics in Russia that they had elsewhere and win the war within weeks or at least before the onset of winter. An equal number of his generals believed that was wishful thinking in the extreme, but, of course, for the most part, they kept that to themselves or among trusted associates.

The progress of the invasion through August and the beginning of September seemed to reinforce Hitler's beliefs. As you can see on the map above, the Germans penetrated deep into the Soviet

Union in the summer and early fall. If you look carefully at the map, you will notice large circles behind the arrows of the German advance. These indicate the surrounded Soviet forces, sometimes numbering almost half a million men or more, and those shown on the map are only the larger examples. Throughout the summer, the Germans, through leadership, fighting skill, and tactics, surrounded astounding numbers of Red Army troops and, in most cases, forced them to surrender. By the end of the campaign in the early winter, the Soviet had lost a million men or more captured, not to mention killed or wounded. It looked as if Hitler was right, once again.

However, the western Soviet Union was not France. Distances were vast, roads were poor if they existed at all, and accurate maps were in limited supply. The front-line combat troops and their vehicles had a difficult time traversing the USSR because of this, and the distances made supplying them a very slow and tenuous thing. The German movement was made worse in the fall (as well as the early spring) by the onset of the rainy season and the *Rasputitsa*- (Russian for "the season of mud").

The vast countryside of the USSR, most of which did not have modern drainage or even trees, to say nothing of the dirt roads, turned into a literal sea of mud twice a year, slowing movement to a crawl. Thus, beginning in the early fall of 1941, the Germans were forced to slow their advance along the entire front. The good news, for the Germans at least, was that the mud froze when the weather got cold, and in late October, the Germans began their march on Moscow once again. Of course, you likely know that it gets very, very cold in Russia.

The delay gave the Russians some time to reorganize, and more importantly, in December, they were able to move reinforcements from the Soviet Far East to the front in the west. The latter was due to Stalin's spies in Japan, whom he now trusted. They had told him that the Japanese were going to attack the United States and that they did not plan to invade the USSR from the east. And on

December 7th, 1941, this was borne out by the Japanese attack on the US Pacific Fleet at Pearl Harbor. This allowed Stalin to move nearly one million trained troops to the front against the Germans, where, on December 5th, the Soviets launched a counterattack outside Moscow and other places along the front, pushing the Germans back over one hundred miles. The Nazis would never come as close to Moscow again, and the Germans' situation was made even worse by Hitler's decision to honor his alliance with the Japanese by declaring war on the United States on December 11th.

The number of Soviet troops took the Germans by surprise. They had already been shocked by the fighting in the summer and fall when it seemed that despite killing and capturing millions of Soviet troops, there were always more to replace them. This time around, at least outside Moscow, many of the replacements actually knew how to fight.

What's more, the Germans were stunned by the number of Soviet tanks they encountered. Most of them were subpar; they were either obsolete or poorly designed. However, two series of Soviet tanks, the KV (Mark I and II) and the T-34, completely took the Germans by surprise. The heavy KV series was able to sustain an incredible amount of damage before being destroyed or breaking down, and though they moved slowly, they packed a powerful punch. The T-34 surprised the Germans even more, and they even forced the most ardent of Nazis to admit that the machine was better than anything the Germans had at the time. Luckily, for the Germans, in late 1941 and early 1942, the T-34 was not rolled out in the incredible numbers that it would be in the latter part of the war. Still, the appearance of these tanks forced the Germans to both revisit their assessment of the Soviets and also hurry to the drawing board to design a tank that could rival the Soviets' machines.

In the spring of 1942, the Germans were no longer strong enough to launch an offensive all along the front as they had the previous year. Despite having defeated the Soviets in most of the battles of 1941 and having stabilized the line after the Soviets' counterattack outside Moscow, German tank forces and manpower were limited. Toward the end of 1942, the Germans would not be able to replace the losses they were sustaining, whereas the Soviets (and, since December, the US) had an almost unending supply of manpower.

The Germans also had a vast empire to defend now. Over the two years, increasing numbers of troops would be sent to guard the French coast. Over 200,000 men were stationed in Norway, for Hitler believed that the British might try to invade the Nordic country once again. Hundreds of thousands of men were stationed in Yugoslavia and Greece, fighting against resistance movements there, and over 100,000 men were fighting the British and soon the Americans in North Africa, not to mention occupation troops throughout Europe. The Soviets, who had more than twice the population of Germany at the beginning of the war, put every eligible man (and, in many cases, boys) into the effort against the Germans.

The German plan for the spring of 1942, dubbed *Fall Blau* ("Case Blue"), called for an armored strike deeper into Ukraine, with its target being the city of Stalingrad (now Volgograd). Simultaneously, they would continue to hold the rest of the Eastern Front and continue to besiege the city of Leningrad (today's St. Petersburg) and strike into the Caucasus in an attempt to seize the vast oil reserves at the city of Baku. Just about one million men and 1,500 tanks would attempt to take the city that bore Stalin's name and cut off the vital Soviet supply line of the Volga River.

The offensive began in late June 1942, and by the last week of August, German troops were fighting in the outskirts of Stalingrad. By the end of September, Hitler's forces held 90 percent of the city, and the Führer announced that the battle was essentially over. However, it wasn't. The Red Army, digging in and under orders to fight to the death, had stiffened their resistance the farther the

Germans penetrated into their country. They held that last 10 percent of the city while sustaining and inflicting incredible casualties in what might perhaps be the most brutal street fighting of the war.

Some Soviet reinforcements were sent over the Volga River under almost constant attack by German planes. A plan developed in the Soviet General Staff, calling for just enough troops to be sent into Stalingrad to be able to hang onto the foothold they had in the center of the city along the river. The rest of the reinforcements would be sent to the fronts in the north and south of the city under cover of darkness to wait until the order to attack was given. The placement of Soviet troops was no accident. Aside from being strategically brilliant, the Axis troops to the north and south of the city were mostly Hungarian, Romanian, and Italian troops, whose hearts were not at all in the fight. This was made worse by enmity between the Germans' allies and their poor equipment.

By mid-October, the temperatures in the Soviet Union had begun to drop, as had increasing amounts of snow. Amazingly, the Germans, who had a bad experience during the previous winter in Russia, were still not equipped with enough winter clothing. By November 19th, when the Soviet counterattack known as Operation Uranus began, temperatures were falling far below zero and would drop to as low as -40ºF for much of the winter.

Within days, the Soviet counteroffensive had broken through the weak lines to the north and south of the city and surrounded the German 6th Army. Though Hitler insisted that the city would and could hold out, most of the generals in the German Army knew that was impossible. An abortive relief effort began some days after the Soviet attack, only to be stopped after about a twenty-mile advance.

For the Germans inside Stalingrad, it was only a matter of time before the end, which came in late January and early February 1943. For the month and a half they had to wait, they suffered frostbite and the lack of food, medicine, and warm clothing. The horses they had brought with them were killed for food shortly after the Soviet attack. Soon, the men were eating rats, if they ate at all. When the Germans at Stalingrad surrendered, ninety thousand men went into Soviet captivity. Five thousand survived to return to Germany about ten years later.

Stalingrad was a pivotal point in the war. Though the Germans would mount one more major attack at Kursk in July and a number of local counterattacks, for the most part, Hitler's forces were on the defensive in the east for the rest of the war.

Stalingrad cost over a million Soviet and German lives. The entire war in the Soviet Union and on the Eastern Front during the war cost the Soviet more than twenty million people, both military and civilian. It would not end until the Soviet's Hammer and Sickle flag flew over the Reichstag building in Berlin.

Of course, this is just an overview of the war, both in the east and in the west. For a more detailed study of the war between Hitler and Stalin, please see Captivating History's *The Eastern Front*, available on Amazon.

The War in the West

While Hitler and Stalin were fighting to the death in the Soviet Union, the war in North Africa and the Western Front continued, though in a much different form, at least from 1941 to late 1942.

In 1941 and 1942, the British stood alone against Hitler in the west, and though they sometimes engaged in heavy fighting in the North African desert to prevent Hitler from capturing the vital supply line that cut through the Suez Canal, the war on the Western Front was limited to the Battle of Britain, which continued in fits and starts through the spring of 1942, the commando raids on the French and Norwegian coasts, and the Battle of the Atlantic.

The Battle of the Atlantic was the only thing that truly frightened Winston Churchill throughout the war, for if the British did not win the battle on the ocean, Britain would starve and run out of enough arms to defend itself.

From 1940 until late 1942, the German U-boat offensive took a great toll on British and Allied shipping, at one point leaving Britain with only enough food to feed itself for two weeks. Fortunately, the British were helped in their struggle in several ways.

First, they had a massive navy with experienced crews and leaders motivated by the desire to keep their country free. Second, they developed and refined a tactic that had proved useful to them during WWI, that of the convoy system, in which fast anti-submarine vessels would escort large numbers of merchant ships across the Atlantic. Third, they developed sonar, which allowed them to search the ocean depths for U-boats rather than rely on seeing or detecting them with radar at the surface, which often proved too little, too late. Fourth, the British, in one of the war's most secret efforts, began to break German codes, especially naval codes, in a top-secret project called "Ultra." Many times, from 1942 onward, the British knew where German submarines were before the German High Command did.

Lastly, the British were aided by the United States. Even before the Americans' entry into the war in December 1942, they were escorting merchant convoys halfway across the Atlantic and "handing them off" to the British, who would take them the rest of the way. Hitler ordered his submarines to refrain from attacking American and neutral shipping in the western Atlantic, and despite a couple of isolated instances, this held. It seemed the last thing Hitler wanted was a war that included the United States, which makes his declaration of war on America on December 11th even more inexplicable.

America's massive industrial complex had begun to ramp up even before its entry into the war, and the nation supplied Britain with weapons, ammunition, planes, tanks, ships, fuel, food, and much else. By the time the war ended, the United States would become the richest and most powerful nation known in human history, possessing the largest industrial plant in the world, a navy many times larger than even the Royal Navy, twelve million men under arms, and the sole ownership of the atomic bomb.

However, in late 1941, that was a long way away. The United States' entry into the war and their insistence on doing things "their own way" cost them millions of tons of shipping sunk off the coast of the United States in what the German U-boat crews called the "Second Happy Time" (the first being the beginning of the war).

Additionally, when US troops did enter combat against the Germans at Kasserine Pass in Tunisia in February of 1943 after the Anglo-American invasion of North Africa, the quality of their troops, tanks, and leadership was brought into question after a hard defeat at the hands of Erwin Rommel.

Still, they learned fast, and with the additional strength of their navy and increasing numbers of merchant ships bringing troops and supplies to Europe, overwhelming the relatively small number of U-boats in the Atlantic, the strength of the Americans increased by the day, as did the British and their Imperial forces.

In July 1943, just days after Hitler launched his last major counterattack in the USSR at Kursk, the British and Americans invaded the Italian island of Sicily, forcing Hitler to order troops to Italy when he could not spare them after the defeats he had sustained in Russia.

In September 1943, the Allies landed in multiple places on the Italian coast, and though the fighting was incredibly difficult (much more difficult than had been thought), British and American troops fought their way to the gates of Rome in the first week of June 1944.

Rome itself was liberated on June 5th, 1944. It was a great victory that was overshadowed by what happened the next day in France: the D-Day landings.

All the while, the Allies had been mounting ever-stronger bombing attacks against German cities and industries. This campaign, which would eventually destroy every major German city, was costly, with the Germans fighting with both fighter planes and tens of thousands of anti-aircraft guns. In both the British and American armed forces, no branch sustained more deaths as a ratio of its strength than the air forces.

With the successful Allied landing on the French coast on June 6th, 1944, Hitler's fate was sealed. If the Allies had failed on the Western Front, he would've had the ability to move many hundreds of thousands of troops to the Eastern Front before the Allies were able to mount another effort. What might have happened if these German troops had been moved to the Eastern Front has been debated since 1945. Would Hitler have been able to defeat Stalin? It is doubtful, especially when you consider the size of the Red Army and the fact that the United States was still developing the atomic bomb, but at the very least, the war would've been prolonged, and hundreds of thousands or perhaps millions more people might have died.

As it was, it took a Herculean effort for the Allies and the Soviets to drive into Germany in 1945. In the east, the Germans inflicted many more times the number of casualties on the Soviets as the Soviets did them. In the west, the limited size of the front condensed German manpower and firepower; at times, for instance, in the late fall of 1944, the front resembled that of WWI to a degree (for those interested, look up the Battle of the Hürtgen Forest). Hitler was also able to secretly amass a quarter of a million men for his Ardennes Offensive in December (also known as the Battle of the Bulge) and launched thousands of the first ballistic rockets in history at Great Britain, Holland, and Belgium. What's more, despite the massive Allied bombing campaign, German industrial output actually increased in 1944, though that was temporary.

Still, the end was inevitable. Though Hitler survived an assassination attempt on July 20th, 1944, on April 30th, 1945, ten days after his fifty-sixth birthday, he committed suicide in his underground bunker in Berlin, spending his last days in madness and delusion. On May 8th, 1945, the German High Command surrendered to the Allies, and German history would enter a new phase.

Illustration 39: Last known picture of Adolf Hitler, at the entry to his bunker; Berlin, 1945.

Chapter 10 – The Holocaust

During the war, trains, men, and much materiel were used by the Germans to transport and kill the Jews of German-occupied Europe rather than utilize them in the war effort. Since the end of the war, historians have studied this and have come to essentially the same conclusion: the extermination of the Jews was more important to the Nazis than actually winning the war. In more than a few instances, German troops that were needed immediately at the front lines had to walk or wait while hundreds of trains transported Jewish people to the camps.

That sounds heartless, but it is the truth. To Hitler and Himmler, their deaths were more important than the war at the front. In the twisted minds of Hitler, Himmler, and the Nazi true believers, the "threat" that the Jews posed for Germany and Europe was greater than the threat posed by the war.

However, though the Germans developed a reputation for efficiency during the war, a deeper look into the German war effort shows that the Nazis were not as efficient with their resources and manpower as one might think. The example above comes to mind, but two other examples illustrate the point well.

In February 1943, after the defeat at Stalingrad had been announced to the nation, Propaganda Minister Josef Goebbels stood in front of a packed house of thousands at the Berlin Sportpalast and gave one of the most rousing and intense speeches of the Nazi era. The people in the audience went wild. At the end of his long speech about the war and its causes, he asked the crowd and the millions listening on the radio, "Do you want total war? If necessary, do you want a war more total and radical than anything that we can even imagine today?" He was pumping up the crowd, but he also had extolled them to work fourteen-, sixteen-, and twenty-hour days for the war effort. There were still areas of the German economy that were not at full capacity, as 1944 would show.

The other example that shows how inefficient the Nazis could be was the V-1 and V-2 efforts. Instead of developing those weapons, the Nazis could have built five more battleships, thousands of more tanks and planes, and much else. Hitler insisted on their development, even though they carried only a bit more than most conventional bombs, were wildly inaccurate, and did not even dent the Allied war effort. Had the Germans built one or two good all-purpose tanks, planes, or vehicles rather than a huge, highly technical assortment like they did with the materiel that went into the V-program, the war truly might have ended differently.

However, the war against the Jews increased full steam from the late 1930s onward, and it never stopped. In actuality, most of the six million Jewish victims of the Holocaust had been murdered by the end of 1944, with the peak of the killing having been reached between the years 1942 and 1944.

Before we begin, let's make one thing clear. Though the Jews were by far the largest group singled out by the Nazis, there were others. It is estimated that a further two million Roma, homosexuals, Jehovah's Witnesses, political prisoners, and others died in the camps. This figure does not include the Russian prisoners of war who died by the millions in German captivity, which are estimated to be over three million. Though most of these victims died in prisoner-of-war camps or in the field, it should be noted that the first victims of the Auschwitz gas chambers were Soviet prisoners of war.

Previously, we told you of *Kristallnacht*, the Night of the Broken Glass, in Germany and many of its consequences. The persecution of the Jews in Germany accelerated after *Kristallnacht*. Within days, the requirement of the German Jews to transfer all retail businesses to Germans was issued. This included mom-and-pop stores as well as department stores, a particular enemy of the Nazis and many of which were Jewish-owned. Department stores, as the Nazi thinking went, lowered prices on the same goods sold by the "more traditional" local shop, which the Nazis saw as a stable of village and town life, never mind that small Jewish shop owners were sometimes affected by this as well.

A few days after this, all Jewish children and young adults were expelled from German schools. The worst insult took place on December 12th, 1938, when it was ordered that the Jews of Germany pay for the property damages that occurred during *Kristallnacht*.

The Holocaust is, unfortunately, a broad subject, and we can only touch upon it here, but at this point, the main purpose of the Nazi persecution of the Jews in Austria and Germany seems to have been to force the Jews out of the country. However, that was fraught with problems. The Jews were required to pay enormous sums for exit visas, money that most did not have. In addition, the offices handling the exit visas and other paperwork were understaffed and moved at a glacial pace. Also, sadly, many Jews believed that the worst of the persecution was over and that life would soon return to somewhat "normal" after Hitler solidified his power.

Perhaps worst of all was the lack of cooperation and the willingness to take Germany's Jews among the other countries of Europe and the United States. The Swiss, where many desired to go, requested the Germans stamp German-Jewish passports with a "J" so they could restrict the number of Jews coming into their country. Poland, which was once one of the most accepting countries toward Jewish immigrants in the past, was at the same time extremely anti-Semitic; almost twenty thousand Polish Jews living in Germany were expelled shortly before *Kristallnacht* but were refused entry into the country. Nearly nine thousand of them were stranded in a border village until the beginning of the war the following year. Other nations of Europe had quotas on both immigration in general and Jews in particular, but it should be noted that Holland and France did take sizable numbers of German Jews.

Sadly, a strain of anti-Semitism ran deep through the US Department of State, which, at the time, dealt with international matters, including refugees and immigration. The State Department had an immense influence on President Franklin Delano Roosevelt, who was from the same social strata and ethnic background as many leading State Department figures and harbored some of their anti-Semitic beliefs as well, though he did include Jewish-Americans in his inner circle. The most infamous incident occurred in June of 1939 when the ocean liner *St. Louis* arrived off the coast of Miami, carrying some nine hundred Jewish refugees, and was refused entry. To be "fair," the ship was also denied entry into Cuba and Canada, though several countries did negotiate with the Jewish Joint Distribution Committee, a humanitarian organization, which still exists today, for cash payments to take in a number of the *St. Louis's* Jewish refugees. Sadly, the ship eventually returned to Europe, and most of the remaining Jews on board (254 of them, including young children) were eventually killed by the Nazis.

On January 30th, 1939, in a speech to the Reichstag commemorating the Nazis' seizure of power, Hitler uttered the words that many believe directly pointed to the future. In his speech, he said, "if war erupts, it will mean the extermination of European Jews."

At the time, very few outside Germany believed this literally, thinking it another of Hitler's ranting speeches, but inside the Reich, the words of the Führer were gospel. Those outside Germany couldn't fathom the possibility of killing *all* the Jews of Europe. To people in Hitler's inner circle who brought up the subject, he simply replied, "Who, after all, speaks today of the annihilation of the Armenians?" History forgets that German General Liman von Sanders played a supporting role in the Turks' persecution of the Armenians during WWI.

Hitler's goal before the war seems to have been the expulsion of the Jews from Germany or German-controlled territory. However, that goal was made virtually impossible by the German conquest of Poland in 1939. The pre-war Jewish population of Poland was about three million, more than four times the size of Germany's 700,000. Indeed, more Jews lived in Poland than any other European nation. With the addition of Polish territory in 1939 and eastern Poland in 1941 during Operation Barbarossa, Hitler increased the number of Jews under his control manyfold.

This was the beginning of the Nazis' earnest conversation to begin some sort of "Final Solution to the Jewish problem," which was what the Nazis later euphemistically called the murder of millions of innocent people.

Inside Poland, as in Germany, the Jews tended to live in their own neighborhoods in cities and towns. In smaller villages and the countryside, everyone knew who the Jews were, even if they were not distinguishable by their unique clothing, as many Jews in Eastern Europe were. Also, within Poland, as in Germany, Jews, generally speaking, had particular names with particular spellings and were kept track of by the authorities. When the Germans moved in, it was a relatively simple matter for them to identify and round up Poland's Jews. In many cases, Jews were ordered to assemble at a specific place at a specific time or face serious consequences. In this, the Nazis were aided by anti-Semitic Poles or Poles who simply wanted to "get in good" with their new rulers.

Within a relatively short time, the Jews of German-controlled Poland had been herded into small and grossly overpopulated sections of the major Polish cities into what were called ghettos. "Ghettos" is actually a word of likely Italian origin, meaning "foundry," as the first "ghetto" was said to be around a forge in Venice in the 1600s. Soon, the ghettos of Poland were being crammed with additional refugees from Germany, Austria, and Czechoslovakia.

Almost immediately, the Germans set up a program designed to kill the Jews in the ghettos by neglect. Food was at a minimum, and it was frequently rotten. The crowded conditions overwhelmed what sanitation and water systems did exist, and diseases of all kinds ravaged the population, as did starvation.

When the Germans invaded the Soviet Union, they realized that it would be impossible to house the nearly three million Jews of the Baltic states and the Soviet Union in the ghettos of Poland. Before the invasion, Himmler and his righthand man, Reinhard Heydrich, the head of the SD, had their subordinates organize "special action groups" (*Einsatzgruppen*) to "deal with" the Jews they found as they followed the front line troops.

The commanders of the *Einsatzgruppen* were SS officers, and while many of the men of these special action groups were also SS men, there were many who were not. They were generally older men from the *Ordnungspolizei* or "Order Police," the uniformed police of Germany. Christopher Browning's best-selling and well-regarded bestseller *Ordinary Men: Reserve Police Battalion 101 and the Final Solution in Poland* describes these men as, well, "ordinary." They, by and large, were not men with delinquent records or histories of brutality. Most of them were lower-middle-class career policemen with a high school or sometimes a college diploma, yet they engaged in one of the worst atrocities that mankind has ever known.

Another historian named Daniel Goldhagen, in his *Hitler's Willing Executioners*, makes the argument that these men were not "ordinary" but conditioned by years of anti-Semitism in Germany, both before and during Hitler's reign. Both Browning and Goldhagen, as well as others, argue that the perpetrators of the Holocaust and other crimes against humanity since then were encouraged by the fact that their actions were "legal" or commanded, thereby abstractly "giving them permission" to murder.

Throughout 1941 and early 1942, the *Einsatzgruppen* fanned out over the Baltic states and then the Soviet Union, carrying out massacres in what has lately been labeled "the Holocaust by bullets." At Babi Yar on the outskirts of Kiev (Kyiv), Ukraine, they gunned down over thirty thousand people in plain sight of onlookers. At Rumbula Forest in Latvia, an estimated twenty-five thousand Latvian and other Baltic Jews were gunned down and buried in huge pits. This occurred in smaller numbers (sometimes dozens, sometimes hundreds, sometimes thousands) throughout the Baltic states and the western Soviet Union. Even today, people are discovering previously unknown mass-killing sites in Ukraine.

Illustration 40: Map of the Jews killed in the Baltic states and the western USSR, with the total of those murdered next to the site. This map was submitted by Einsatzgruppe "A" commander Franz Stahlecker. Note that Estonia is labeled Judenfrei—"free of Jews."

From the Nazi viewpoint, there were several problems with this method of eliminating the Jews. First, it was very public; on a few occasions, onlookers from the non-Jewish population saw the killings firsthand. Unfortunately, many of them also took part, which the Nazis were all too willing to allow. Related to this, a number of German soldiers took photos and home movies of the slaughter and mailed them home. Since the war, several undiscovered photo albums have been discovered by relatives in attics and basements after the deaths of their older relatives.

Second, in the eyes of the Nazis, the system of hunting down and killing the Jews was inefficient. Having them "voluntarily" rounded up for "resettlement in the east" was more effective and less likely to cause rebellion and/or panic.

Third, Himmler, though he wasted no tears on the Jews and others whose deaths he was ordering, was concerned about the psychological effect of these mass killings on his men. Though this reason has often been pushed aside among historians, especially in light of the suffering inflicted on their victims, this was a concern for Himmler and the SS leadership. Cases of alcoholism, suicide, and mental breakdown among the personnel of the *Einsatzgruppen* grew dramatically as time went on.

All of these, but particularly the last, were the impetus behind the construction of gas chambers at existing and partially built camps in Poland.

The camps themselves and their method of killing by gas have a tragic prelude within Germany. In a program known as T4, the Nazis began to kill off patients in mental hospitals throughout Germany in the late 1930s. This was done by using poison gas, with the patients under the illusion that they would be taking a shower, or by lethal injection. In six camps in Germany and Austria, the mentally challenged, the insane, and people with severe epilepsy were killed by physicians and nurses, who were supervised by SS officers. The parents or relatives of the victims would receive a letter stating that their loved one succumbed to natural causes, such as a heart attack or stroke.

These "mercy killings" were an open secret, and they were protested by a variety of people, most notably the bishop of Münster, August von Galen, who publicly condemned them and caused them to be halted, albeit temporarily. The general lack of outcry among the German public, however, caused the Nazis to believe that little if anything would be said about the deportation of the Jews "to the east."

The first extermination camp was located at Chelmno (known by the Germans as Kulmhof), near the city of Lodz in western Poland. There, victims were brought to the large former estate of a Polish nobleman. And there, they were killed by asphyxiation caused by the pumping of carbon monoxide exhaust from large trucks. This account by SS sergeant Walter Burmeister after the war explains what happened:

> As soon as the ramp had been erected in the castle, people started arriving in Kulmhof from (Lodz) Litzmannstadt in lorries...The people were told that they had to take a bath, that their clothes had to be disinfected and that they could hand in any valuable items beforehand to be registered. When they had undressed they were sent to the cellar of the castle and then along a passageway onto the ramp and from there into the gas-van. In the castle, there were signs marked "to the baths." The gas vans were large vans, about 4-5 metres [13-16 ft] long, 2.2 metres [7.2 feet] wide and 2 metres [6.6 feet] high. The interior walls were lined with sheet metal. A wooden grille was set into the floor. The floor of the van had an opening which could be connected to the exhaust by means of a removable metal pipe. When the lorries were full of people, the double doors at the back were closed and the exhaust connected to the interior of the van.

—Walter Burmeister, *The Good Old Days*

The bodies would then be trucked to a nearby forest and burned. An estimated 150,000 to 200,000 people were killed at Kulmhof, but Himmler and others considered it inefficient, and they thought the same of the murders at Belzec, north of Lwow (over 600,000 victims), and Majdanek, south of Warsaw (80,000 victims).

At Treblinka and Sobibor, both Jews and Red Army prisoners were killed. Many of the killers were Ukrainian collaborators who blamed Jews for the hated Soviet communist regime in their home country. At both Treblinka and Sobibor, the killing was done by piping in carbon monoxide exhaust from captured Soviet tank engines. This reduced the time it took to kill the prisoners when compared to the other camps at Belzec, Kulmhof, and Majdanek. Additionally, experience with killing in large numbers had essentially created experts in mass murder, and, especially at Treblinka, the time from arrival to one's death was about an hour. Deportees would arrive at a fictional train station, equipped with a painted clock that never moved, and then driven up to a large field surrounded by guards, dogs, and barbed wire. Though they were treated roughly, they were told they were being sent to the showers, and from there, they would be given work assignments. Treblinka was the home of the horrific "tube" (*Schlauch* in German), which funneled naked prisoners through a camouflaged, barbed-wired path leading to the gas chambers. Inside the tube, they would be whipped and beaten like animals, having no idea what lay in store for them. Minutes later, they would be dead, their bodies then transported to open pits crisscrossed with steel railroad ties. This place was euphemistically called "the grill" by the guards. There, specially chosen workers would throw bodies on the ever-burning pyre. In many cases, those who did not move fast enough were kicked or thrown onto "the grill" alive.

Despite Treblinka's death toll of nearly one million people and Sobibor's 625,000 people, Himmler and his SS cronies believed that the killing process could be both more efficient and "more humane" for their guards. Sobibor was eventually shuttered after a mass revolt by Soviet prisoners of war, which resulted in the deaths of SS guards and the escape of many of the rebelling prisoners.

The result of Himmler's insistence on efficiency was the notorious death camp at Auschwitz-Birkenau. Birkenau was actually the second of three camps at the Polish town of Oswiecim. Auschwitz I had been built shortly after the invasion of Poland and housed political prisoners, habitual criminals (who were used by the SS to keep the other prisoners "in line"), members of the Polish resistance, intellectuals, and others. Even before the erection of Auschwitz-Birkenau, Auschwitz I built a notorious reputation for cruelty—the list of diabolical types of physical and mental abuse doled out there would take up pages.

Auschwitz III, or Auschwitz-Monowitz, was located to the east of the main camp in a factory complex converted by the Germans into a lab and factory for the study and production of synthetic resources like oil and rubber. Thousands were worked to death at Monowitz, and not a single effective materiel was ever produced there.

The largest part of the Auschwitz complex was Auschwitz II Birkenau (*Brzezinka* in Polish for "place of birches," named for the birch groves that grew there and which were often the waiting places for people when the gas chambers were "too busy"). Building began at Birkenau in the fall of 1941, shortly after the beginning of Operation Barbarossa.

As was mentioned previously, the first victims of the gas chambers were Soviet prisoners of war in late August 1941 in a small chamber at Auschwitz I. These were the first victims killed using prussic acid, chemical pellets that turned to gas when exposed to oxygen and sold under the now-infamous name of Zyklon B, which had previously been sold to kill rats and other vermin. The killing time of Zyklon B was about fifteen minutes compared to the half-hour to an hour it took using carbon monoxide.

A second and larger gas chamber was built in the spring of 1942, just outside the gate of the camp, which underwent rapid construction. The first gas chamber was built inside a farmhouse, from which the owner had been expelled. It could fit eight hundred people inside at one time. It was deactivated after the construction of the larger three gas chambers inside the camp, which could hold two thousand people at a time.

These new gas chambers could kill so rapidly that specially designed crematoria had to be designed to dispose of the bodies. However, the death toll was sometimes so high that burn pits were used at Auschwitz as well. The pits were also used when crematoria broke down or were destroyed, as happened during a prisoner's revolt on October 7th, 1944. A movie based on this revolt, *The Grey Zone*, is listed in the bibliography at the end of this book (it is for mature audiences only).

At its peak, Auschwitz-Birkenau was killing an estimated twelve thousand to fourteen thousand people a day. Most of the murders at Auschwitz took place from 1942 to 1943, though a new high was reached in the summer of 1944 when Hitler's Hungarian allies, who had been reluctant to send their Jews into German custody (more out of a question of national sovereignty than for any love of their Jewish population, at least among the fascist-dominated government), sent over 400,000 people to their death by allowing the Germans to transport them to Auschwitz.

(The story of Auschwitz is long and brutal, and this e-book is meant as an introduction to German history, not a history of the camps. Please see the bibliography at the end of this book for some authoritative and exhaustive reading on this topic.)

As the war turned against the Nazis and they were forced to retreat toward Berlin, they made attempts to destroy the evidence of their crimes. In places like Babi Yar and Rumbula, surviving Jews were made to dig up what remains were left intact and burn them on large pyres, sometimes fueled by cranes or bulldozers dropping bodies onto them. The intense heat was too much for people to approach.

Though there were six extermination camps—Auschwitz, Treblinka, Sobibor, Kulmhof, Majdanek, and Belzec—there were hundreds of concentration camps throughout the German Empire where death took place on a massive scale, usually by working inmates to death, disease, or starvation. As the Soviets approached from the east and the British and Americans from the west, some of these camps were destroyed. Others, like Belsen or Buchenwald, among others, were left intact by fleeing guards. Battle-hardened troops from the liberating armies were reduced to dumbfounded tears at the sight of the dead, the remaining gas chambers, and the starved skeletons of the living. In many cases, SS members who could not flee attempted to disguise themselves as inmates. Many of them were beaten to death or severely injured by the inmates themselves. In at least one case, twenty-five to thirty-five captured SS guards were openly gunned down at Dachau by the liberating US troops, though this news was suppressed for decades. Only the Russians know how many guards were killed in the east, but unfortunately, many of the executioners, their leaders, or their enablers escaped judgment, either through suicide or by a world unwisely wishing to put an ugly chapter behind it with the coming of the Cold War.

Illustration 41: Image taken by SS guard of the "selection" of victims for the gas chambers at Auschwitz, likely summer 1944. Notice the smoke from the crematoria in the background.

Chapter 11 – Post-War Germany to the Present Day

Alfons Heck, the Hitler Youth member that was mentioned in a previous chapter, was among those Germans fortunate enough to have survived the war. He was one of the young men you see in one of the last pictures of Hitler outside his bunker; he was being given an award for bravery from the Führer himself. Even after the death of Hitler had been announced, Heck and millions like him were true believers. In a prisoner-of-war camp after the ceasefire, Heck and other boys were shown films of the concentration camps, with piles of bodies stacked like wood or strewn about the grounds. Heck and the other boys began to snicker and thought, "Who do they take us for? This stuff is staged!" With that, their guards lit into them, beating them with fists and truncheons and telling them, "You damn Nazis! This is what you've done!" It was not until Heck saw his Hitler Youth leader, Baldur von Schirach, on trial at the Nuremberg trials that he started to believe that the Holocaust had actually happened. And this was only because he heard it directly from his leader and other top Nazis on trial for their crimes against humanity.

Other Germans did not take so long to believe, for the Allies marched local civilians through the camps to see what Nazism and the support of Nazism had done. In many cases, German civilians and surviving guards were forced to bury the thousands of bodies lying about.

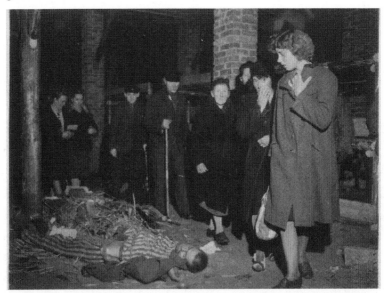

Illustration 42: German civilians marched through the Neuengamme camp near Hamburg by the US 82ᵈ Airborne Division.

As Heck had, Germans throughout the country were sometimes "required" to attend screenings of newsreels of the Nuremberg trials. What they didn't see and hear, they read in Allied newspapers and the many free German newspapers that quickly sprung up.

The Nuremberg trials were important for several reasons. First and foremost, they showed the world exactly what happened under Hitler. Second, it was done as a hopeful deterrent to anyone so inclined to engage in atrocities in future years. Third, it was a punishment, plain and simple. At the Tehran Conference in 1943, Joseph Stalin had half-kiddingly proposed killing a random fifty thousand German officers as a lesson and as a punishment. It is true that great numbers of German officers and soldiers disappeared into the Soviet Gulag camp system, never to be seen again. However, British Prime Minister Winston Churchill and US President Franklin Delano Roosevelt pushed Stalin into holding the Nuremberg tribunal as a public exhibition of Nazi horror and Allied power.

Nuremberg was chosen purposely. It was where Hitler and the Nazis held their huge rallies every year, and by holding the trials here, it was a very clear sign that those days were not only over but were never coming back.

The first of the Nuremberg trials included some of the most famous names in the Nazi world. Unfortunately, both Hitler and Himmler had escaped justice by committing suicide. Reinhard Heydrich, who had been ordered to implement the "Final Solution to the Jewish problem" in Europe by Himmler, had been assassinated in Czechoslovakia in 1942. However, Hermann Göring, who was once Hitler's number two man and the head of the *Luftwaffe*, was captured. In addition to his other duties, Göring had signed off on some of the most important documents and orders that put the Holocaust into motion.

Among the others at the trial were Albert Speer (Hitler's architect and eventual minister of munitions), Field Marshal Albert Jodl (a *Wehrmacht* yes-man at the head of the General Staff), the aforementioned Baldur von Schirach, Karl Dönitz (the head of the German Navy and Hitler's successor after he received word about Göring attempting to make peace without his authorization), Rudolf Hess (Hitler's "deputy Führer" until he flew to England in 1940 in a bizarre attempt to make peace), and about a dozen others. Of the twenty-two defendants in the first round of trials, twelve were sentenced to death by hanging, three were given life sentences, four were given sentences of ten to twenty years in prison, and two were found not guilty. Hermann Göring, due to either a security lapse or with the aid of a sympathetic American guard, was able to cheat the hangman by ingesting a cyanide pill in his cell. Martin Bormann, the head of the Reich's Chancellery and Hitler's secretary, was tried in absentia and sentenced to death; his remains were found in the 1980s in Berlin, and they were confirmed to be his in the 2000s. The trials at Nuremberg and several other places, both in the west and the east, continued for a number of years.

The question facing the world was what should be done with Germany. One American plan floated during the war by Roosevelt's Secretary of the Treasury Henry Morgenthau Jr. (who himself was Jewish and had helped (or attempted to help Jewish refugees before, during, and after the war), developed the Morgenthau Plan for post-war Germany. Put simply, the Morgenthau Plan would have reduced the size of Germany, removed all industries, and created a new and unarmed state of farmers who would be unable to go to war ever again. Given the nature of the Nazi regime, the Morgenthau Plan underwent serious consideration, but in the end, it was refused.

It was refused because the Allies had seemed to learn their lesson after the disaster that was the Treaty of Versailles. Not only would it be practically impossible to force the Germans to become farmers for who knows how many years in the future, but when they began to rebuild, once again, there would be tremendous resentment, just as there had been in 1918, which was something the Allies wished to avoid at all costs.

More importantly, however, were the geopolitical developments taking place in Europe and around the world after the war. By the end of 1945 and into 1946, the Soviets, despite their promises to hold free, fair, open, and democratic elections in the nations occupied by their troops, were already celebrating communist victories in every country in Eastern Europe, with the exceptions of Yugoslavia and Albania, which had largely liberated themselves and were determined to be independent. (Stalin, for his part, knew that the Yugoslavs had fought over half a million Germans during the war largely on their own and would not stand for Soviet interference. And to get to Albania, the Soviets had to go through Yugoslavia.)

While the Western Allies had made promises to the various Eastern European governments in exile in the West, which were mostly democratic in nature, the Soviets had their own Polish, Czech, Bulgarian, Romanian, and Hungarian governments in exile, which were all communist. More importantly, in their home countries, those coming from the West-leaning governments in exile were either refused entry or "disappeared" into the Gulag on their return home. The fact is, short of war, there was nothing the Allies could do to affect anything the Soviets were doing in Eastern Europe.

After the ceasefire, the wartime Allies (the US, Britain, and France in the west and the USSR in the east) had hoped that a united Germany, one neutral in outlook, could be reconstructed, but both sides held suspicions of each other and of the Germans, which kept that from becoming a reality. The division of Germany, which had been devised during the war, was to be a permanent thing.

From 1945 to 1949, Germany was divided into four zones of control: the American, Soviet, British, and French. The capital city of Berlin was likewise divided into four areas.

Illustration 43: The division of Germany between the Allied Powers, 1945 to 1949. The striped Saarland was administered by all four nations.

Western Germany began rebuilding itself almost as soon as the war ended. American and British soldiers could not get over the speed with which the Germans began to clean up and rebuild, and truth be told, they got, for the most part, a much better reception in Germany than they did in many of the lands that had been occupied by the Germans.

By 1949, it was clear that the differences between the Soviet Union and the Western powers were too great to be surmounted. As if basic political differences were not enough, in 1948, Stalin ordered the blockade of Berlin in an attempt to either force the Allies out of the city or to the negotiating table where he could dictate the terms. Russian tanks and troops blocked the roads leading from the western zones to the east, and they threatened to fire on anyone attempting to run the blockade.

However, blocking a road and shooting down a plane are two entirely different things, and the United States decided to call the Soviets' bluff by beginning an airlift into Berlin, bringing the food, fuel, and every other good, as well as personnel, needed to keep the city alive and running efficiently. No one, especially not the Russians, believed the US and its allies—mostly the British—would be able to bring in enough supplies for Berlin to keep from starvation, much less thrive.

Western Berlin needed 4,500 tons of food and fuel *daily* to survive, and while it took some time to reach that goal, it was reached much more quickly than even the Allies believed, and what's more, it was exceeded by a fair amount. It was exceeded to the point that one American transport pilot flew extra sorties over the city and dropped candy to waiting children. His nickname was "The Candy Bomber." At the height of the airlift, a plane was reaching Berlin *every thirty seconds*.

The Berlin Airlift lasted for nearly a year until Stalin relented and opened the roads. The airlift was a public relations disaster for the Soviets, who were having trouble keeping famine at bay in their own war-ravaged country, much less in Eastern Europe.

Not only did the Berlin Airlift bring in food, fuel, clothing, and much more, it also brought hope and tremendous regard for the Allies, especially the Americans who flew the bulk of the flights. The Germans also knew that over one hundred British and American airmen had died trying to keep their city alive. What's more, many Berliners were employed during the period, and they were able to keep themselves warm and full during a very trying time.

Illustration 44: One of the famous pictures from the Berlin Airlift in which German children watch the landing of an American C-54 bringing in supplies to the surrounded city.

In 1949, with increasing tensions between the Allies and the Soviet Union in what was supposed to be a joint administration of Germany, including not only the blockade but also the introduction and success of the new currency in Western Germany, the failure of Eastern Germany to make the same progress and the Soviet attempts to pressure Western German politicians culminated in the announcement that a new country, the Federal Republic of Germany (*Bundesrepublik Deutschland* or "BRD"), was going to be established in the west on May 23rd, with the western city of Bonn as its capital.

In October, the Soviets announced the establishment of the German Democratic Republic (*Deutsche Demokratische Republik* or "DDR") in the east. Berlin was divided between the west and the east, with the DDR naming the eastern half of the city as its national capital.

Throughout the 1950s and 1960s, West Germany underwent what is called the "German economic miracle." From a nation that had been totally defeated and most of its cities completely destroyed, the West Germans, with significant help from the United States in the form of the Marshall Plan, began rebuilding their economy to the point that, by the early 1960s, it was rivaling France as an economic power.

The dominant political party was once again the SPD (Social Democratic Party), but at times, it was forced into coalition governments with the CDU (Christian Democratic Union, a conservative party based in the south) or the Liberals. The first West German chancellor, Konrad Adenauer (1876–1967), known as *Der Alte* ("the old one"), was from the CDU, and he governed the country from 1949 to 1962. The best-known post-war chancellors of Germany are Adenauer, Willy Brandt, Helmut Schmidt, Helmut Kohl, and Angela Merkel, who has announced her retirement after over fifteen years in office as of this writing in 2021.

In 1955, West Germany joined NATO, the North Atlantic Treaty Organization, which was first put together to defend Western Europe from the Soviet Union. In response, the Soviets admitted a newly rearmed East Germany into the Warsaw Pact, its organization to defend itself from an attack from the West.

Western Germany soon became known for its liberal and vibrant political life, as well as a booming cultural life, which included film, music, literature, and art. In some ways, life in West Germany, at least culturally and especially in Berlin, resembled the Weimar period, with the people once again enjoying the freedom of expression after the Nazi era.

Conversely, in East Germany, life stayed hard, and it remained that way. The one-party system under the Socialist Unity Party (*Sozialistische Einheitspartei Deutschlands* or "SED," which was really the "Communist Party" by another name) mirrored Stalin's Soviet Union: repressive and economically backward. Cultural life was dictated by the party, and deviation from it was punished in many ways, including incarceration, forced employment or unemployment (depending on the situation), and social ostracism. Watching its citizens was the Stasi, the secret police ("Stasi" is an acronym of the *Ministerium für Staatssicherheit* or "Ministry for State Security"), which was a little less brutal than the Gestapo. A little.

Life in East Berlin was so miserable and the future so bleak that between 1945 and 1961, tens of thousands of East Berliners defected every year. Between 1960 and 1961, this became thousands every month. Until 1961, East Berliners had the ability to cross into West Berlin, more or less, at leisure, but for the most part, they did not work there. They could see the freedom and economic success of the West firsthand, which was exactly the opposite of what SED propaganda told them it was like. Facing an exodus of labor and intelligence, the East German government, at the strong "urging" of the Soviet Union, took drastic measures to stop the flood and limit contact with the West.

Virtually overnight, on August 13th, 1961, the Berlin Wall went up. At first, it consisted of cinder blocks topped with barbed wire running just inside the East German border. This was done so, in theory at least, East German guards could go over the wall and still be within East Germany to retrieve the dead or those wounded while attempting escape. At first, the border was relatively porous, and people literally broke their legs jumping from buildings overlooking the wall into West Germany. Soon, however, the authorities moved everyone out of the border buildings and bricked up the windows.

When the Berlin Wall was finished, it was hardly made of cinder blocks. Most of it consisted of a ten-foot smooth concrete wall with smooth cement "rollers" on the top, both of which made the wall hard to climb. Of course, to get to the wall, one had to first get by several security checkpoints, floodlights, barbed wire, police dogs, minefields in ever-changing places, ditches, and more. The Berlin Wall didn't just divide Berlin; it was erected down the main East and West German border, and it went on for hundreds of miles.

I personally visited Berlin twice during the Cold War, in 1980 and 1981, legally crossing into East Germany on my first trip. The Berlin Wall was not only physically but also psychologically daunting, and East Berlin was an experience in what can best be called "greyness"—it was a city that seemed to have a pall over it even on a sunny day. When myself and two friends responded to the smiles of a group of young people in a park near the wall, we were soon stunned by the rapidity with which they dispersed. Unseen by us, a group of police (known as "VoPos" for *Volkspolizei* or "People's Police") had approached. The East German teenagers fled like a school of startled fish before we knew the police were even around, as they did not want to be seen talking to Americans.

Despite the daunting obstacles, many East Germans escaped or attempted escape from the repression in their home country. An estimated total of over five hundred people was killed trying to escape East Germany, one not long before the wall came down in 1989. Over five thousand people did manage to escape, however. Some literally climbed over the wall. Many tunneled underneath it.

A few even used makeshift hot air balloons to cross. The ways in which people in East Germany escaped are amazing, and many of their stories are told in the Haus Am Checkpoint Charlie Museum, which is still standing in Berlin and has a great online presence.

When Mikhail Gorbachev became the premier of the Soviet Union in 1985, he almost immediately signaled that many changes would be coming to the Soviet Union and the nations of the Warsaw Pact (or Eastern Bloc). Gorbachev realized that the Soviet system was not creating the "socialist paradise" the regime had been promising for decades. Actually, during most of the 1960s through the mid-1980s, the Soviet economy stagnated due to the lack of economic freedom and technical skill, as well as having been forced to compete with the United States in the arms and space races, something which was hitting new heights under President Ronald Reagan.

Gorbachev announced two new massive policy shifts: *perestroika* and *glasnost* ("restructuring" and "openness," respectively). The Soviet economy would be reconstructed to become more efficient and competitive, and the government would be more open with its people about what was truly happening in the country (this last policy was spurred on by the Chernobyl nuclear disaster). While he was at it, Gorbachev "suggested" that the nations of Eastern Europe adopt these changes as well, something many of its rulers were not inclined to do. What's more, Gorbachev announced the USSR would not be able to send economic aid to its allies any longer, as it was barely getting on by itself.

For the leaders and regimes of Eastern Europe, this was the end. Without Soviet aid and Soviet soldiers, their unpopular regimes would fall, and in 1989, that was exactly what happened. Throughout Eastern Europe, "people power" successfully and peacefully, apart from Romania, overthrew their governments or forced them to slowly change from within.

East Germany's leader at this time, Erich Honecker, was among the most hardline communist leaders and actually contemplated firing on the many demonstrations that were taking place within his country, as had been done in 1953 when East German workers went on strike; hundreds, perhaps more than a thousand, were killed. But times were different. Not only would many of Honecker's generals not support this order, but the Soviets also made it clear that they might actually interfere should this begin.

At the end of October and the beginning of November, the East German government slowly then rapidly came apart. Amazingly, on another November 9th in German history, the Berlin Wall fell. Less than a year later, East Germany voted itself out of existence and united with its western counterpart. Germany was one again.

Illustration 45: East and West Germans on the now-defunct Berlin Wall, 1989.

Conclusion

In the years since the reunification of the country, the Germans have had to face a variety of problems. The first one was the absolute poverty of East Germany. Over the years, billions of marks have been allocated to help support and train Eastern Germans while they helped build and form a modern economy, build new infrastructure, and integrate East Germany into the fold.

This has not been without problems. In West Germany, significant resentment against the "hand-outs" given to the *Ossis* (a play on the German word for "easterners") built up. Conversely, those in East Germany felt that the *Wessis* (a play on the word for "westerners") were snobs and looked down at those in the east. Additionally, many in the east found the world of cutthroat capitalism in the western half difficult and repulsive, while westerners saw the easterners as without ambition. Despite the passage of time, some of these attitudes still exist.

Worse still, with the end of the East German police state under communism, old hatreds and bigotries, having been suppressed but not addressed, have reared their ugly head in the form of neo-Nazism and racism in what was once East Germany. What's more alarming is that this was seen as mostly an *Ossi* problem until recently.

Because of its WWII history, West Germany has felt a particular need to help in humanitarian causes throughout the world but especially in Europe. One that made headlines was the German-led bailout of Greece in the early 2000s when the latter country was on the verge of economic collapse.

In 2011, Germans took refugees from the Arab Spring uprising in the Middle East, and in 2015, Chancellor Angela Merkel allowed hundreds of thousands of Syrians fleeing the civil war in their country into Germany. Germany had been a refuge for those fleeing war and persecution for years, and, in the case of Germany's large Turkish population, it was partly done for economic gain. In recent years, Germany has taken in more refugees than any other country.

While most Germans have been welcoming, an increasing number have called on a moratorium or a law to limit the number of foreigners allowed into the country. Several attacks on German women by Arab youths alarmed the country, as have increasing numbers of right-wing attacks on Arabs by Germans. A new party, known as the *Alternativ für Deutschland* ("Alternative for Germany" or "AFD"), which at times uses rhetoric very similar to that of the 1930s, has gained influence. Its presence, along with popular support for limiting refugees, has caused a shift to the right in Germany, which has alarmed some.

Still, every year, Germany ranks among the wealthiest, happiest, healthiest, and most free nations on Earth, which is a far cry from 1945.

Here's another book by Captivating History that you might like

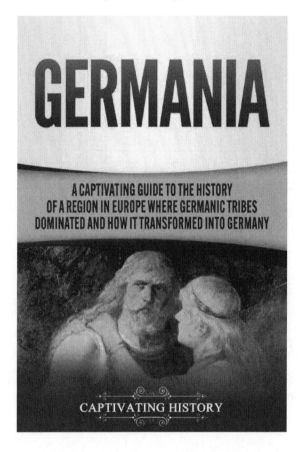

Free Bonus from Captivating History
(Available for a Limited time)

Hi History Lovers!

Now you have a chance to join our exclusive history list so you can get your first history ebook for free as well as discounts and a potential to get more history books for free! Simply visit the link below to join.

Captivatinghistory.com/ebook

Also, make sure to follow us on Facebook, Twitter and Youtube by searching for Captivating History.

Bibliography/References

BABYLON BERLIN. Directed by Henk Handloegten, Achim Von Borries, and Tykwer Tom. Berlin: Netflix, 2017.

Browning, Christopher R. ORDINARY MEN. New York: HarperCollins, 2013.

CAPTIVATING HISTORY, THE TREATY OF VERSAILLES: A CAPTIVATING GUIDE TO THE PEACE TREATY THAT ENDED WORLD WAR 1 AND ITS IMPACT ON GERMANY AND THE RISE OF ADOLF HITLER. Captivating History, 2020. Available on Amazon.com.

Crankshaw, Edward. BISMARCK. London: A&C Black, 2011.

Dear, Ian, I. C. Dear, and M. R. Foot. OXFORD COMPANION TO WORLD WAR II. Oxford: OUP Oxford, 2001.

Deighton, Len. WINTER. London: Penguin Classics, 2020.

Evans, Richard J. THE COMING OF THE THIRD REICH. London: Penguin, 2005.

Evans, Richard J. THE THIRD REICH AT WAR: HOW THE NAZIS LED GERMANY FROM CONQUEST TO DISASTER. London: Penguin UK, 2012.

Evans, Richard J. THE THIRD REICH IN POWER. London: Penguin, 2006.

THE FIRST WORLD WAR. Directed by Hew Strachan. n.d. Hamilton Film, 2002. DVD.

Freedman, Russell. WE WILL NOT BE SILENT: THE WHITE ROSE STUDENT RESISTANCE MOVEMENT THAT DEFIED ADOLF HITLER. Boston: Houghton Mifflin Harcourt, 2016.

Gaskill, Matthew. THE GERMAN ARMY AND STORMTROOPERS OF WORLD WAR ONE: TACTICS OF TERROR. Nashville: Amazon, 2014.

Goldhagen, Daniel J. HITLER'S WILLING EXECUTIONERS: ORDINARY GERMANS AND THE HOLOCAUST. New York: Vintage, 2007.

Haffner, Sebastian. DEFYING HITLER. Plunkett Lake Press, 2019.

THE GREY ZONE. Directed by Tim B. Nelson. 2001. Film.

"HOME." WALL MUSEUM - MAUERMUSEUM - MUSEUM HAUS AM CHECKPOINT CHARLIE - STARTSEITE. ACCESSED MAY 5, 2021. HTTPS://WWW.MAUERMUSEUM.DE/EN/START/.

HOLT, A., & HOTTUM, R. (DIRECTORS). (1991). HEIL HITLER! THE CONFESSIONS OF A HITLER YOUTH [FILM].

HEIMAT (PART I). Directed by Edgar Reitz. 1984. Berlin. Film.

Hilberg, Raul. THE DESTRUCTION OF THE EUROPEAN JEWS. Google Print Common Library, 2003.

Holmes, Richard, Hew Strachan, Chris Bellamy, Hugh Bicheno, and Professor of the History of War and Fellow Director Oxford Program on the Changing Character of War Hew Strachan. THE

OXFORD COMPANION TO MILITARY HISTORY. New York: Oxford University Press, USA, 2001.

"How Many Refugees Came to the United States from 1933-1945? - Americans and the Holocaust - United States Holocaust Memorial Museum." Online Exhibitions — United States Holocaust Memorial Museum. Accessed May 4, 2021. https://exhibitions.ushmm.org/americans-and-the-holocaust/how-many-refugees-came-to-the-united-states-from-1933-1945

"Introduction to 19th-Century Socialism." Common Errors in English Usage and More. Washington State University. Last modified October 12, 2016. https://brians.wsu.edu/2016/10/12/introduction-to-19th-century-socialism/.

Isherwood, Christopher. THE BERLIN STORIES. New York: New Directions Publishing, 2008.

Johnson, Eric A. NAZI TERROR. New York: Basic Books (AZ), 1999.

Junger, Ernst. STORM OF STEEL. *(PENGUIN CLASSICS DELUXE EDITION)*. London: Penguin, 2016.

Kershaw, Ian. HITLER: A BIOGRAPHY. New York: W. W. Norton & Company, 2008.

Lowe, Keith. SAVAGE CONTINENT: EUROPE IN THE AFTERMATH OF WORLD WAR II. New York: St. Martin's Press, 2012.

MacMillan, Margaret. PARIS 1919: SIX MONTHS THAT CHANGED THE WORLD. New York: Random House, 2007.

MacMillan, Margaret. THE WAR THAT ENDED PEACE: THE ROAD TO 1914. New York: Random House, 2013.

Musolff, Andreas. "Wilhelm II's 'Hun Speech' and Its Alleged Resemiotization during World War I." Welcome to UEA Digital Repository - UEA Digital Repository. Accessed March 27, 2021.

https://ueaeprints.uea.ac.uk/id/eprint/65777/1/Accepted_manuscript.pdf.

Neitzel, Sonke, and Harald Welzer. SOLDATEN - ON FIGHTING, KILLING AND DYING: THE SECRET SECOND WORLD WAR TAPES OF GERMAN POWS. New York: Simon & Schuster, 2012.

Nelson, Anne. RED ORCHESTRA: THE STORY OF THE BERLIN UNDERGROUND AND THE CIRCLE OF FRIENDS WHO RESISTED HITLER. New York: Random House, 2009.

Noakes, Jeremy, and Geoffrey Pridham. DOCUMENTS ON NAZISM, 1919-1945. New York: Viking, 1975.

Rhodes, Richard. MASTERS OF DEATH: THE SS-EINSATZGRUPPEN AND THE INVENTION OF THE HOLOCAUST. New York: Vintage, 2007.

Röhl, John C. KAISER WILHELM II: A CONCISE LIFE. Cambridge: Cambridge University Press, 2014.

"The Royal Navy in WW1." Naval Encyclopedia. Last modified June 18, 2020. https://www.naval-encyclopedia.com/ww1/royal-navy-1914.

Sandford, John. ENCYCLOPEDIA OF CONTEMPORARY GERMAN CULTURE. London: Routledge, 2013.

Sarotte, Mary E. 1989: THE STRUGGLE TO CREATE POST-COLD WAR EUROPE - UPDATED EDITION. Princeton: Princeton University Press, 2014.

Shirer, William L. THE RISE AND FALL OF THE THIRD REICH: A HISTORY OF NAZI GERMANY. 1980 edition.

"Treblinka: Revealing the Hidden Graves of the Holocaust." BBC News. Last modified January 23, 2012. https://www.bbc.com/news/magazine-16657363.

Weitz, Eric D. WEIMAR GERMANY: PROMISE AND TRAGEDY, WEIMAR CENTENNIAL EDITION. Princeton: Princeton University Press, 2018.

Wetzel, David. A DUEL OF GIANTS: BISMARCK, NAPOLEON III, AND THE ORIGINS OF THE FRANCO-PRUSSIAN WAR. Madison: University of Wisconsin Press, 2003.

Printed in Great Britain
by Amazon